INTERRUPTING INNOVATION

INTERRUPTING INNOVATION

CENTRING THE SOCIAL

EDITED BY

**MELANIE PANITCH
SAMANTHA WEHBI
JESSICA PIMENTEL MACHADO**

Copyright © 2025 Melanie Panitch, Samantha Wehbi and Jessica Pimentel Machado.

All rights reserved. No part of this book may be reproduced or transmitted in any form by any means without permission in writing from the publisher, except by a reviewer, who may quote brief passages in a review.

Development Editor: Fiona Jeffries
Copyediting: Karen May Clark
Cover Design: Jess Koroscil
Text Design: Brenda Conroy
Printed and bound in the UK

Published in North America by Fernwood Publishing
2970 Oxford Street, Halifax, Nova Scotia, B3L 2W4
Halifax and Winnipeg
www.fernwoodpublishing.ca

Fernwood Publishing Company Limited gratefully acknowledges the financial support of the Government of Canada through the Canada Book Fund and the Canada Council for the Arts. We acknowledge the Province of Manitoba for support through the Manitoba Publishers Marketing Assistance Program and the Book Publishing Tax Credit. We acknowledge the Nova Scotia Department of Communities, Culture and Heritage for support through the Publishers Assistance Fund.

Library and Archives Canada Cataloguing in Publication
Title: Interrupting innovation : centring the social / edited by Melanie Panitch, Samantha Wehbi and Jessica Pimentel Machado.
Names: Panitch, Melanie, editor | Wehbi, Samantha, editor | Pimentel Machado, Jessica, editor.
Description: Includes bibliographical references and index.
Identifiers: Canadiana 20240539001 | ISBN 9781773637297 (softcover)
Subjects: LCSH: Social change. | LCSH: Social systems—Growth. | LCSH: Social justice. | LCSH: Social action.
Classification: LCC HM831 .I56 2025 | DDC 303.4—dc23

To Leo Panitch,
whose intellectual and political optimism embraced us
and recognized the promise here.

Contents

About The Contributors viii

Acknowledgements xii

1 **Framing Social Innovation as a Call For Social Transformation**
   Melanie Panitch, Jessica Pimentel Machado and Samantha Wehbi 1
   "Follow The Money!" 1
   Social Innovation: Key Concepts and Theoretical Reflections 3
   Structure and Themes 8

2 **Social Innovation Re-Loaded: The Social as Innovation**
   Kiaras Gharabaghi 14
   The Benefits of Social Problems 16
   The Sensory Context of Social Innovation 22
   The Fallacy of the Social Innovator 26
   Conclusion: Re-Loading Social Innovation 30

3 **Pro-Tests and *Making With Place*: Socially Engaged Arts Activisms and Innovations reCentring the Margins**
   Phyllis Novak and Charlotte Lombardo 36
   Socially Engaged Arts and Social Movements —
   What Makes Them So Significant in Propelling Change? 37
   Internal Landscapes in Creative Meaning-Making — Where the Practice
   Movement Begins 42
   Collaborative Activations: MWP and Production as Collective Care 43
   Relational Becoming and Collective Identity — Space For Theorizing Together 47
   Collective Action toward Radical Belonging —
   Is This Not the Ultimate Aim of All Social Movements? 49
   Conclusion 51

4 **Considering Networked Responses as Social Innovation: Case Examples Of Incels and Amazon's Ring and Community Care**
   Lauren Morris, Al Cunningham Rogers and Quinn MacNeil 58
   Theoretical Underpinnings: A Critical Understanding of Social Innovation 61
   Neoliberalism as a Shaping Force 61
   Case Example I: Incels 62
   Case Example II: Amazon's Ring 67
   Case Example III: Care Collectives 72
   Conclusion 77

5　Power Sharing, Community Leadership and Dynamic Governance at The SHIFT Centre for Social Transformation

SHIFT Governance Hub Members Cheryl Gladu, Stephanie Childs, Kristen Young and Katarina Prystay..81

Background and Context..83
Brief Introduction to Organizational Theory and Design.............................85
The SHIFT Centre for Social Transformation 88
Principles and Practices that Guide the Work at SHIFT 93
Case Example: Firsthand Account of SHIFT's Impact 97
Conclusion..101

6　Life Imitates Art: Collage as Innovative Pedagogy

Ken Moffatt and Reena Tandon..105

Theoretical Underpinnings..107
Collage..109
Innovative Teaching and Learning through the Collage Project....................111
Collage as Innovative Pedagogy...117
Conclusion..123

7　The Importance of Justice and Decolonization Questions in Science Education

Brooke Filsinger and Roxana Sühring..126

Introductions..127
Why We Need to Consider Ethics and Social Justice in Chemistry Education 129
Education, Worldviews and the Responsibility of Science.............................131
Critical Thinking...132
Relationship in Science and the Need for Less Objectivity..........................134
Moving From "Can We?" to "Should We?" 136
Moving Science Out of the Vacuum...138
Conclusion..140

8　Innovate for Impact: Unleashing Social Change Through Values-Driven Leadership and Visionary Action

Wilson Leung...142

Discovering Our Core Values 143
Crafting Our Leadership Purpose...145
Identifying Societal Challenges...147
Creating a Vision for Change..149
Turning Vision into Action 151
Exploring a Case Study 153

Glossary 156

Index 161

About the Contributors

STEPHANIE CHILDS has a background in conflict transformation, collaborative decision-making and alternative governance developed over a decade of working in the food movement. In her role as the lead on community engagement and shared power at SHIFT, she prioritizes care and creativity in the co-development of organizational structures that allow insights from diverse perspectives and worldviews to advance work toward a more just and equitable future.

BROOKE FILSINGER is an Indigenous scholar pursuing doctoral studies at Toronto Metropolitan University. Her work focuses on Community-building and space-making for Indigenous Knowledges, pedagogies, and research methodologies within science. She is dedicated to elevating and amplifying Indigenous student voices.

KIARAS GHARABAGHI is dean of the Faculty of Community Services at Toronto Metropolitan University. He spent over twenty years working in various positions in the homelessness, child welfare and mental health sectors. For over ten years, Dr. Gharabaghi has been involved in social innovation theory and practice and has co-developed a minor in the field at TMU.

CHERYL GLADU is an assistant professor of human enterprise and innovation at Thompson Rivers University and an interdisciplinary scholar who studies dynamic systems of governance and innovative approaches to community-led research and development. She became involved in SHIFT while completing her doctorate at Concordia University and is a member of SHIFT's Governance Hub.

WILSON LEUNG is the director of the Graduate Leadership Institute at Toronto Metropolitan University. He is also the vice-president of Global Learning and Leadership Development at Plus Company. Dr. Leung is a certified executive coach and holds a doctorate specializing in leadership. He is passionate in his work to help leaders flourish and communities thrive.

CHARLOTTE LOMBARDO is a community-engaged scholar, educator and facilitator whose practice is rooted in youth empowerment, community arts and participatory research. For over twenty years she has led and collaborated on diverse creative research and action projects for promoting youth voice and cultural leadership and for addressing issues concerning: social and environmental justice; community wellness and health equity; and youth-centred systems and services.

JESSICA PIMENTEL MACHADO has been creating and supporting social innovation initiatives in higher education for nearly ten years. She is a steward with her local union and is involved in grassroots community activism in gender-based and sexual violence. She is pursuing her M.Ed in Adult Education and Community Development at the University of Toronto where her work explores critical pedagogy through coalition-building activities and social movements.

QUINN MacNEIL holds a B.A in Rhetoric and Communications from the University of Winnipeg and an M.A in Communication and Culture from York University. Quinn's research focuses on surveillance, the data economy, visual culture, and discourses of community safety and criminality. She was a co-principal investigator for the project "Deconstructing/Performing the Amazon Ring Security Apparatus" as part of the Office of the Privacy Commissioner of Canada Contributions Program 2022-2023 and continues to critically engage with our entanglement with oligopolies, surveillance, and images in the digital age.

KEN MOFFAT (he/him) is Professor of Social Work at Toronto Metropolitan University (TMU), Adjunct Professor, MacMaster School of Social Work, and the past Jack Layton Chair (Faculty of Arts, Faculty of Community Services TMU, 2018-2022). His research interests include affect, creative arts, and imaginative engagement as well as the limiting effects of capitalism and neo-liberalism on personal expression and well-being. He is the author/editor of Troubled Masculinities: Reimagining Urban Men (2012) and the author of Postmodern Social Work: Reflective Practice and Education (2019). He is the creator of the Podcast on art and social justice, Downstream from What (2023-2024) and Principal Investigator of SSHRC-funded Crafting Community Project and Collective (2022-2024). He loves curating and co-creating queer art spaces in small venues.

LAUREN "L" MORRIS (they/them) is an interdisciplinary artist-scholar, care worker, and community builder from Southern Alberta. For the past ten years, they have supported a variety of queer, feminist, and community-led grassroots initiatives. Their master's research studied 2SLGBTQIA+ and Mad/Disabled community care using community-engaged and art-based methods.

PHYLLIS NOVAK (she/they) is a social arts curator, researcher and strategist, trained in theatre performance with an interdisciplinary arts practice. The founding artistic director of SKETCH Working Arts (1996–2021), she is now working on her PhD in arts and social movements, connecting academic and community activist scholarship in the arts that centres cultural leadership and counter-narratives "from the margins" to make social and environmental change.

MELANIE PANITCH is the executive director in the Office of Social Innovation at Toronto Metropolitan University. Previously she held the John C. Eaton Chair of Social Innovation and Entrepreneurship in the Faculty of Community Services and was the founding director of the School of Disability Studies (1999–2011). Her exhibit, "Out from Under: Disability, History and Things to Remember," is installed in the Canadian Museum for Human Rights. She is the author of *Disability, Mothers and Organization: Accidental Activists* (2008).

KATARINA PRYSTAY is an early career researcher exploring the potential of arts-based community infrastructure development. Her academic background is in theatre and urban planning. She became involved in SHIFT as a research assistant and a member of the Governance Hub.

AL ROGERS is a masculinities and political violence scholar and archivist-in-training. They have a BSS in political science and communications from the University of Ottawa, an MA from Toronto Metropolitan University, and they are attending the University of Toronto's Management Information Systems program. They currently work on SSHRC-funded research on racism, public consultation and the city of Toronto.

ROXANA SÜHRING is an assistant professor in analytical environmental chemistry in the Department of Chemistry and Biology at Toronto Metropolitan University. She holds a doctoral degree of natural sciences (Dr. rer. nat.) in environmental chemistry from the Leuphana University in Lüneburg and conducted postdoctoral research in Germany, Canada and Sweden. From 2016–18, she led a regulatory scientist team at the Centre for Environment, Fisheries and Aquaculture Science. During this time, she also was the policy advisor to the Netherlands' delegation for the OSPAR Offshore Industry Committee regarding offshore chemicals, as well as advisor to the UK's Ministry of Defence regarding potentially polluting shipwrecks. Her interdisciplinary research focuses on understanding the fate and behaviour of emerging contaminants in the environment that originate from consumer products, such as microplastics and plastic additives.

REENA TANDON is an interdisciplinary, community-engaged scholar and practitioner. She leads the Faculty of Arts Community Engaged Learning and Teaching (CELT) initiative at Toronto Metropolitan University. Dr. Tandon has taught at universities in New Delhi and Toronto and was selected as the DiverseCity Fellow by Civic Action, Toronto. She is the co-author of *Immigration and Women: Understanding the American Experience–Finding Agency, Negotiating Resistance, and Bridging Cultures* (2011). Dr. Tandon was a Mellon Postdoctoral Fellow at the Johns Hopkins School of Public Health in Baltimore, Maryland, and held a CIHR Postdoctoral Fellowship at the Centre for Research in Inner City Health at St. Michael's Hospital in Toronto. She received her PhD in social work and social policy from La Trobe University in Melbourne, Australia.

SAMANTHA WEHBI is professor of social work at Toronto Metropolitan University. Her research and artistic practice interests have focused on international issues, grassroots community activism and organizing in Canada and abroad, including Lebanon, her country of origin. Her work has explored the complexities of urban landscapes and issues of displacement, postcolonialism, translocality and social change. Her scholarship explores interdisciplinary intersections of art, community practice and pedagogy. Dr. Wehbi is the co-editor of *Reimagining Anti-Oppression Social Work: Reflecting on Research* and *Re-imagining Anti-Oppression Social Work: Reflecting on Practice* (2017).

KRISTEN YOUNG is a community archivist and records manager currently splitting her time between Tiohtià:ke/Montréal and Tkaronto/Toronto. She graduated with a MISt from McGill University in 2016, and since then has worked in government, private, corporate and community archives. As a Jamaica-born Canadian citizen, she has a vested interest in the Caribbean-diasporic community in Tiohtià:ke/Montréal, working to ensure that Black communities maintain access to their community archival materials through conservation, advocacy and capacity building.

Acknowledgements

As staff and faculty members of Toronto Metropolitan University (TMU), and as settlers to this land, the co-editors would like to begin with TMU's land acknowledgement: Toronto is in the "Dish with One Spoon" territory. The Dish with One Spoon is a treaty between the Anishinaabe, Mississaugas and Haudenosaunee that bound them to share the territory and protect the land. Subsequent Indigenous Nations and Peoples, Europeans and all newcomers have been invited into this treaty in the spirit of peace, friendship and respect.

It is in this spirit of recognition that we would also like to thank the authors whose dedication to progressive practice and critical social thought has deepened what it means to interrupt innovation. Not only have their contributions enriched this volume, but their collegiality and willingness to meet deadlines and engage in revisions have made compiling this book a labour of love. We owe much thanks to Fiona Jeffries, acquisitions and development editor at Fernwood Publishing, for her passionate, tireless and thoughtful accompaniment on this book-writing journey.

Our understanding of social innovation as social justice has been moulded by the creative and risk-taking students, staff and faculty who have worked within and alongside the Office of Social Innovation at TMU since 2018. It was in the fall of that year that then Provost and Vice President Academic Dr. Michael Benarroch gave us the wings to fly, affirming the value of centring the social in social innovation and providing resources to put ourselves on the map. Institutional support has been ongoing, and we are enormously grateful to be working at a university with an aspirational commitment to advance as a change leader for the public good.

Even more personally, each of the editors wishes to say a special thanks to people who have provided support in multiple facets of our lives, supporting our freedom to thrive creatively and to grow in our understanding of social innovation and transformation. Thank you for your support, Vida Panitch, Maxim Panitch, Deirdre Boyle, Scarlet Pollock, Roukie Wehbi, Mahmoud Wehbi, Dr. Bob Cambria, Tim Chan, Marie-Paule Duret, Angela Machado, James Machado and José Pimentel.

Last but not least, please note that some of our authors have chosen to thank specific people or institutional actors for their support at the end of their chapters; we direct your attention there.

Framing Social Innovation as a Call for Social Transformation

Melanie Panitch, Jessica Pimentel Machado and Samantha Wehbi

"FOLLOW THE MONEY!"

A CATCHPHRASE POPULARIZED by the 1976 docudrama *All the President's Men* may seem a curious introduction to a book on social innovation and social justice; however, if you "follow the money!" when it applies to the student debt crisis, you will find you are in the territory of a complex social issue.

Student loans and grants are typically a policy issue, but given the crisis of postsecondary education, scrutinizing the world of student debt for what it can reveal is an instructive entry point to this field. We discovered this when we received an interesting invitation from our university's student financial aid department. It was a call for help from the newly appointed manager of the student financial aid department who was perplexed as to why students were always so upset. As an office of social innovation, we position ourselves to create a space to imagine alternative pathways and perspectives. But student loans? We were intrigued by the question and the unique partnership. Guided by our commitment to collaboration, we became explorers, learning all we could about how student loans work, and so we arrived at the intricate and sometimes murky world of loans and student debt.

We began by meeting with administrators to hear about the complexity of their jobs. We looked into job descriptions, government policies, manuals and regulations; we observed practices and behaviours and located academic research. We learned that our university has the highest take-up of student loans in our province of Ontario; so, this was relevant. Just how relevant became abundantly clear when we hosted a town hall session to hear directly from students about their experiences and their challenges with navigating the financial aid system. Over three hundred of them turned up for an online session and many more participated in focus groups.

The students eagerly shared their thoughts, feelings and concerns. We heard about their anxiety, their insecurity and the inequitable impact of loans. They described the ways financial pressures affect their mental and physical health and academic performance as they try to balance part-time employment, housing and food insecurity. They spoke of the worrisome impact of gateway debt, the ballooning balance of what they will owe when they graduate and how this financial reality of theirs perpetuates social inequality, especially in an environment of high interest rates. We documented through systems mapping and their student voices the nuances and intricacies in an ongoing research study called "Degrees of Debt," itself a methodological innovation as we attempted to report on this issue in a unique way. All of this innovation was sparked by one question from a thoughtful manager who reached out for help. The benefits of this innovative partnership were mutual. The financial aid office gained a deeper understanding of the impact of their work, and our team found a pedagogically relevant case study with which to foster a systems-thinking approach with students concerned about social and environmental issues of social justice.

Excited by the critical discussion on social innovation and transformative social change generated through the case of student debt, we began to search the scholarship for relevant articles and books that might similarly approach social innovation through a social justice lens. While we found that the current scholarship offers much in terms of understanding social innovation, as well as examples of social innovation in practice through case studies and examples, we struggled to find examples that pertained to the Canadian context. This gap is of importance because, as we shall argue in this book, social innovation is contextual, relational and socially located, and thus the sociological and national contexts make a difference in how we understand and see social innovation in action.

Stemming from this desire to find core material of application and interest in the Canadian context, we developed this book as a beginner's guide to the key ideas, thinking and examples of social innovation. Our intention in this book, as the title suggests, is to interrupt the continuity and uniformity of innovation from one that is nebulous and primarily focused on entrepreneurship, the limitations of which we will note later. In addition, we have sought to take this guide one step further so as to anchor it conceptually and practically as a tool and guiding lens to social justice. By interrupting innovation, we have wrestled the social to arrive at centre stage through many manifestations of social life taken up by the authors included here.

Our vision for what is possible is inspired by a poster of Peter Schumann's iconic print, one that we see every day in our workspace, reminding us to engage in "resistance of the heart against business as usual." (See the poster at breadandpuppetpress.org/products/resistance-of-the-heart.)

Beginning in this chapter, we provide readers with key concepts and theoretical reflections to guide understandings of social innovation, specifically as it relates to social justice and transformation. The chapter begins with an overview of the historical and contextual development of social innovation, including a discussion that explores and troubles social innovation through a social justice lens. We then proceed to a discussion of some of the distinguishing features of social innovation when viewed from a social justice perspective. Specifically, we highlight and discuss the following characteristics of social innovation: creative approaches to understanding and addressing social issues and seemingly intractable social problems; sharing and shifting power; forging community partnerships and local networks of change; understanding the historical and systemic nature of injustice; and the role of higher education institutions as a complicated site of, and catalyst for, change. These concepts are illustrated through case studies in the second section of the book. The chapter ends with a discussion of the main themes drawn from these case studies, as well as an overview of the book's structure. We then conclude with some thoughts as to how the book can be used by students and educators.

SOCIAL INNOVATION: KEY CONCEPTS AND THEORETICAL REFLECTIONS

Over the past decade, there has been a rise in interest in social innovation as an approach to tackling systemic social issues in new ways (Moulaert & MacCallum, 2019; Nichols, Simon, & Gabriel, 2018). Nichols, Phipps, Provençal and Hewitt (2013, p. 25) contend that: "Although innovation in science and technology remains critical, there is increasing recognition that *social* innovation is required to achieve sustainable social and economic impact" (original emphasis). Interest in social innovation has led to the growth of social innovation courses, programs and specializations at Canadian, American and European universities. These offerings are currently available through management and business schools, international development programs, community development programs, schools of environmental studies and planning and public policy, to name but a few.

At this time, there is an exciting growth of the scholarship as conceptualizations of social innovation develop across these disciplines and become explored in others. Scholars are deepening their examination of existing approaches to social innovation through the creation of interdisciplinary sub-fields, such as in creativity, governance and socio-political movements (Moulaert & MacCallum, 2019; van der Have & Rubalcaba, 2016). Critical perspectives of social innovation are also emerging in the scholarship and are addressing issues of power relations that have long been ignored — a significant example being Goodchild's (2021) exploration of decolonizing systems thinking and awareness. Goodchild uses the visual code of the Two-Row Wampum belt to invite us into a sacred space of "non-interference in between [Indigenous and non-Indigenous] epistemologies" (p. 99). Because of the importance of relationality and context to social innovation, critical perspectives are necessary in addressing the problematic components of the field.

The predominant conceptualizations of social innovation have aligned it with entrepreneurship (Baldarelli & Del Baldo, 2016; Dey & Steyaert, 2016; Duarte Alonso, Kok, & O'Brien, 2020; Farinha, Sebastião, Sampaio, & Lopes 2020). However, social innovation is a growing field with multiple approaches, mandates and applications not solely tied to conceptions of entrepreneurship (Teasdale et al., 2020). Moreover, as Addo (2017) notes, assumptions of social innovation tied to entrepreneurship are implicitly based on conceptions of the formal market economy that do not take into account racialized and gendered engagement in informal economies. Similarly, an entrepreneurship lens on social innovation has been challenged to recognize unique understandings of entrepreneurship as tied to values, history, place and colonial and precolonial contexts for Indigenous communities (Mika, Warren, Foley, & Palmer, 2018).

As well, alignment with the concept of entrepreneurship in a neoliberal capitalist economy often moves away from the effort to challenge and shift power that is necessary for social transformation. It is especially problematic when this discourse absorbs social innovation — for instance, when "social entrepreneurship" and "social innovation" are used similarly or interchangeably — because it depoliticizes social innovation. Alternatively, this discourse may lead toward charitable models trying to attempt social change, which also fails to address the conditions that are ultimately creating precarious situations for communities (e.g., in housing, employment and healthcare). The authors in this book instead illustrate community-based examples of social innovation that align with building collaboration, solidarity and coalitions for social change.

In recognition of the intractability of social problems and the limits of entrepreneurial conceptions of social innovation, scholars have called for looking beyond defining and framing social innovation as individualized, "virtuous citizenry" (Slee et al., 2021, p. 793) or as the "charitable dimension of the concept" (Batle, Orfila-Sintes, & Moon, 2018, p. 15), both of which have tended to reproduce existing social power relations. Departing from these entrepreneurial approaches, this book adopts a conceptualization of social innovation aligned via social justice. We define social justice as a process and a goal which seeks the full and equitable participation of all in a mutually shaped society. Defining social innovation as a social justice process and goal requires us to emphasize the key concepts of creativity, collaboration, systemic change and engagement, as discussed below.

Creative approaches are necessary in developing our understanding and addressing complex social issues. Several chapters in this book engage with creative approaches to problem identification and proposed responses; they also discuss the process of teaching and learning about social innovation. We take up artistic expressions of creativity, as well as engagements with various cultural spaces and forms, as a means to bring about important conversations that contribute to our understanding of social innovation. We believe that the importance of creativity and its integration in the understanding of social innovation lies in its long history of being inextricably linked to social transformation through protest and other forms of community mobilization for social justice (Kester, 2011; Reid, 2005; Thompson, 2012). Creative approaches hold the potential to not only interrupt the status quo but to also provide a vision for what could be possible. As such, creativity is fundamental to understanding and responding to social issues and to building a vision of social transformation.

Indeed, van der Have and Rubalcaba (2016) have identified a strong interdisciplinary scholarly community in social innovation with a focus on creativity research. In these studies, researchers and practitioners are interested in the process-oriented questions of how new ideas and new social relationships can be organized to create social transformation. Considering creativity in a conceptualization of social innovation that is aligned with social justice invites us to identify, question and challenge our sources of creativity. Which relationships and environments encourage us to imagine and think in creative ways? What conditions build and expand our capacity for creativity? Where do we feel supported to attempt creativity and to learn from those messy endeavours? What limits and restrains our creativity?

One of the recurring concepts in social innovation that demonstrates the necessity of creativity is the "wicked problem." Coined by Rittel and Webber (1973) and introduced in the context of social policy, the "wicked problem" identifies an issue that is seemingly intractable and extremely difficult to solve. Common characteristics of a wicked problem include aspects of it that are incomplete, contradictory and constantly changing. Importantly, Rittel and Webber use the word "wicked" to denote the problem's resistance to resolution. Widespread social issues like poverty and homelessness are referred to as wicked problems. Often, a wicked problem is usually a symptom of other wicked problems too: while poverty itself is a wicked problem, it is also a symptom of homelessness and vice versa. Wehbi et al. (2023) note how wicked problems tend to drive social innovation because their systemic nature and immense complexity demand creative and collaborative approaches. Significantly, working through these wicked problems toward social justice requires strategies to share and shift power.

Avelino (2021) discusses how the notion of power is taken up in social transformation and social innovation literature and identifies common contestations of power, such as: power "over" versus power "to"; consensual versus conflictual; and constraining versus enabling. One of the most significant contestations is the relationship between power and knowledge — the extent to which power defines knowledge and the role of power in creating, manipulating and disseminating knowledge. It is crucial to understand the dimension of power and how it can be shared and shifted because it is an inevitable and necessary aspect of transformative change. Creatively addressing wicked problems will require attempts to challenge, alter and even replace dominant social power relations and institutions.

The scholarship also explores and documents case studies that demonstrate the negative sides of social innovation that emerge through failed attempts — attempts that often disrupt and destabilize communities and end up reproducing existing power relations. While illustrating this outcome in the context of renewable energy transitions and energy justice, Pel et al. (2023) interpret and position various outcomes of the negative sides of social innovation. One spectrum ranges from naïve optimism to paralyzing critique (e.g., from disavowing a negative side as an incidental setback to the exaggeration and de-legitimization of efforts). Another spectrum ranges from intended to unintended consequences (e.g., from purposive harm to unexpected outcomes). With such high stakes in attempting social innovation, it is of the utmost importance to become aware of potential harms and other negative outcomes.

Sharing and shifting power, specifically with and toward communities that have been severely impacted by oppression and injustice, requires forging community partnerships and local networks of change. Efforts in social innovation must be informed and led by those most affected, and who are the most familiar with the depth and complexity of a wicked problem and the actions necessary to sustain social change. Case studies of social innovation processes demonstrate different levels of community relationships, often ranging from consultation to cooperation, as demonstrated by the authors in this book. Confronting the power relations and institutions that uphold and benefit from the persistence of wicked problems requires strong and trusting relations with affected communities. Creating these local networks moves beyond short-term collaboration efforts and toward politicized engagement. It is necessary to consider political action within a social innovation process when we centre community relationships that are developed with the goal of social justice. As such, there are opportunities for social innovation to engage community-led efforts of solidarity, coalition building and social movements since these are pathways into social transformation.

As we engage in relational work with these communities, there is an important responsibility for understanding the historical and systemic nature of injustice. Rayner and Bonnici (2021, p. 32) describe that "the most successful examples of social change focus on the process itself, ensuring that systems become *responsive* and *representative*, with learning at the heart of the change process" (original emphasis). Without community leadership and careful consideration in the design of a social innovation process, efforts can easily reproduce or worsen the same tensions, conflicts and relations that are causing a wicked problem to persist. Often, discrimination and exclusion are embedded in the ideological roots of these wicked problems and are manifested through oppressive systems such as colonialism, racism, sexism, classism and ableism. It is expected that this ongoing learning journey is difficult as it also requires us to be aware of our own positionality. Campbell and Eizadirad (2023) suggest that learning and dialogue around social justice must occur in a space that is supportive and kind and allows for calculated risk-taking in questioning historical and dominant institutions and discourses. Understanding the depth and complexity of injustice through multiple perspectives can expand our insight and capacity for imagining alternative and new possibilities and futures.

With a traditional mission in teaching and research, Higher Education Institutions (HEIs) are well-positioned to foster these spaces and mobilize scholarship for social change. Scholars in social innovation often debate the role of these institutions. Milley et al. (2020) note that in a Canadian context, most HEIs engage in mentorship and capacity-building activities in social innovation, with half of these activities comprising entrepreneurial endeavours (e.g., supporting venture creation and commercialization). Under decades of federal, provincial and territorial policies of neoliberal austerity, HEIs have been under immense pressure to seek out and create revenue-generating opportunities in order to sustain their traditional activities which have come at the cost of their integrity: international students are exploited through soaring tuition fees and institutions are now invested in venture creation and commercialization activities (Kwong, 1993). As a result, HEIs are even more problematic as being sites of social change and social transformation. As they move toward resembling and becoming corporate and private entities, HEIs reproduce the same dominant interests and power relations.

Hence, eschewing simplistic and uncomplicated understandings of social innovation, we embark on a journey of exploration of the contours of social innovation as connected to the pursuit of social transformation with the authors of each chapter. The book, as a whole, explores the questions, struggles and experiences of conceptualizing and practicing social innovation as an endeavour of collective action. In line with social innovation thinking that begins with redefining the key questions, the exploration in this book is guided by such questions as: Can social innovation be conceptualized and practised in a way that is socially transformative? Is it possible to take up social innovation in a way that dismantles harmful and exclusive systems while avoiding cooptation? What is the role of social innovation in sabotaging and resisting neoliberalism in our institutions, communities, partnerships and personal lives? What does social innovation mean and look like within community participation, artistic engagement and radical direct action? Importantly, how does exploring these questions influence pedagogy and praxis in social innovation? In this context, the ambiguity that marks theorizing and defining social innovation can be celebrated as it opens up many opportunities to integrate social innovation in interdisciplinary ways.

STRUCTURE AND THEMES

The book began by providing readers with key concepts to guide their understanding of social innovation, specifically as it relates to social justice and transformation. What will follow are five chapters that detail various case examples from the Canadian context which will allow readers to understand how conceptualizations of social innovation through a social justice lens can be applied to systemic issues. Drawn from disciplines such as chemistry, social work, psychology, sociology, art-making and community practice, the examples provide key reflections and analyses of social innovations and highlight several interconnected themes. Throughout the volume, common ideas among the chapters are cross-referenced. Readers may follow up on the ideas presented in one chapter by reading complementary ideas in other suggested chapters. We have also included a glossary of key terms at the end of the book; when these terms first appear in the book, they will show up in bolded text.

The first theme is that social innovation actions create new spaces to think, reflect and develop solutions to long-standing social issues. In Chapter 6, Reena and Ken demonstrate how **collage** is used to help students break out of the confines of traditional learning spaces in order to create new solutions and responses to social problems, such as racism, heterosexism and other forms of marginalization. Similarly, in Chapter 3, Phyllis and Charlotte discuss socially engaged art practices as a way of reframing and reclaiming public space so as to tackle longstanding social issues. The key here is to engage with action beyond a focus on analysis, thereby creating "new paradigms for intervention, which address root causes of social problems rather than the symptoms" (Nandan, London, & Blum, 2014, p. 66). Activities such as collage or community interventions that alter the landscape require us to think through ideas about social change in a concrete way, creating an alternative space where we can dream and bring into being a different reality.

The second theme considers using the goal of social transformation to reorient our thinking. This is innovative because though we may begin with the familiar goal of attaining social justice, what is required is not only action but a change in our thinking. In Chapter 2, Kiaras lays the groundwork for this rethinking through a discussion of what we mean by the "social" in "social innovation." Thinking through a different understanding of the concept, Kiaras teaches us how to move to a fuller comprehension of how solutions can also work to address social transformation for the most marginalized, rather than serving only to eradicate social problems.

Furthermore, in Chapter 7, Roxanna and Brooke challenge us to rethink how we understand a traditional academic discipline such as chemistry from a social transformation perspective that would value and be inspired by Indigenous ways of being and knowing. Along the same vein, Stephanie and her colleagues discuss in Chapter 5 a shift in thinking in terms of governance and the opportunities for collaborative leadership that this shift can bring about. Their example allows us to see how an alteration in thinking about the role of higher learning impacts social change outside the confines of the academic institution. This change is facilitated through co-creation by creating not only links to the community but also by modelling inclusionary decision-making and community-development practices. As Kumari et al. (2020, p. 4) note, co-creation is at the "core of the social innovation process." This type of rethinking dictates new priorities and asks new questions about age-old practices and institutions.

A related theme is that social innovation reminds us to look at the world around us in new ways. Social media, consumer culture and corporate influence have become routine aspects of our everyday. A critical understanding of social innovation allows us to rethink how these practices can be a detriment to the health and well-being of our communities. We see this theme reflected in Chapter 4 by Lauren, Al and Quinn through their critical analysis of social media, technological advances and social policy changes; in three case studies, they illustrate how social innovation can either be detrimental or how it can be leveraged to allow for social transformation.

A fourth theme is that of the impact of **neoliberalism**. Often associated with economic policies of privatization, free trade, austerity and reductions in government spending on public works in order to increase the role of the private sector in society, neoliberalism and its policies have increased economic inequality, giving rise to socio-economic insecurity and alienation. It is a field ripe for social innovation. Further, neoliberal thinking prioritizes quantifiable factors such as economic indicators of growth and inflation over social factors such as community-building, labour rights and access to education. When the discourse of innovation is rooted in neoliberal ideology, we can see its impact in higher education: the commercialization of knowledge; the strengthening of ties to the private corporate world; the reductions in funding; the calls for efficiencies; and standardization via benchmarks and performance indicators (Moffatt, et al., 2016). The individual actor in this perspective is one who is self-defined, autonomous and competitive; and one whose self-interest is elevated over social need.

Pushing back against this neoliberal framing, Kiaras asserts the fallacy of the solitary social innovator or heroic entrepreneur in Chapter 2. Likewise, Lauren and colleagues, in Chapter 4, illuminate through their case example of a surveillance approach to community safety, how in practice it leads to individual silos, disempowering community members from building deeper relations with one another. Countering the rugged individualism embedded in neoliberal thought, the authors in this book celebrate a critical understanding of responsibilization, a process in which individuals working collectively at the grassroots, outside of traditional structures and institutions, are able to exert influence over their own social well-being and that of their community.

A final theme is that of the need to transform ourselves, so we can contribute to social transformation in the world around us. Social innovation takes up ideas of leadership in a way that promotes authentic leadership to support the union of personal and social transformation. Lawrence, et al. (2018, p. 636) invite us to consider that "leading includes the whole person, beyond a set of skills, competencies and knowledge." In Chapter 8, Wilson incorporates these ideas of leadership by engaging readers with reflection activities to think about how they could move their social innovation vision further and how they can integrate social innovation thinking in their frame of reference. Scholars have noted the urgency of integrating leadership and social innovation as both reinforce each other in the search for systemic responses to societal problems (Nandan, London, & Blum, 2014; Stauch, 2016). Starting with a vision of change, ethical guidelines and self-awareness, Wilson's contribution offers a space for reflection and skill development so as to enhance leadership potential that can, in turn, contribute to meaningful change.

We have provided a space to go well beyond highlighting the 'social' in social innovation, reflecting the maturity of the field in research and practice. All of the authors here have problematized, critiqued and challenged narrow conceptions of social innovation that relegate it to a limited understanding of entrepreneurship in sharing their experience to answer one of the guiding questions outlined earlier: Can social innovation be conceptualized and practised in a way that is socially transformative? We have taken "the small initiatives that have the greatest potential to foreshadow by persuasive example, the transformation of those arrangements and that consciousness" (Nichols, Simon & Gabriel, 2018, p. 234). The extent to which power is shifted in favour of a disadvantaged group is the key test for social innovation as social justice. All the authors have addressed this and made manifest in their analysis how their initiatives have delivered on that front, delivering a social good that includes, for example, resources, water, accessibility, decision-making, education and the opportunity to be heard.

What is core to the work of social change but not always recognized as central to the discussions and debate is the extent to which social innovation is the work of the heart as well as the mind. A sense of passion as a driver for change is less prominent in the social innovation literature but it is very much present in practice as can be seen in this book; the social innovators, scholars and practitioners writing here are driven, often tirelessly, by their own experiences and their commitment to making the world a better place. In their work and in their research, they have made a place for art, creativity, imagination and a sense of adventure. They are not objective and aloof, and they certainly are not dispassionate observers—they are very much inside the frame.

We invite you to find your own way into this frame!

Reflection Questions

1. Thinking about this chapter's discussion of "wicked social problems," what are some such issues that you can identify in your community? Which ones do you feel a passion toward addressing?

2. What causes "wicked social problems" to persist? Why do you think these issues have existed for so long? Who stands to benefit from these wicked problems continuing to persist?

3. How does creativity manifest in your life? How can it contribute to social transformation in your community?

REFERENCES

Addo, P-A. (2017). "Is it entrepreneurship, or is it survival?": Gender, community, and innovation in Boston's Black immigrant micro-enterprise spaces. *Societies, 7*(3), 1–19.

Avelino, A. (2021). Theories of power and social change: Power contestations and their implications for research on social change and innovation. *Journal of Political Power, 14*(3), 425–448.

Baldarelli, M-G., & Del Baldo, M. (2016). Ethics, gift and social innovation through CSR and female leadership in business administration in Italy. *uwf UmweltWirtschaftsForum, 24*(2-3), 141–150.

Batle, J., Orfila-Sintes, F., & Moon, C. J. (2018). Environmental management best practices: Towards social innovation. *International Journal of Hospitality Management, 69*, 14–20.

Campbell, A.B., & Eizadirad, A. (2023). Cultivating brave spaces to take risks to challenge systemic oppression. In A. Eizadirad, A.B. Campbell, & S. Sider (Eds.), *Counternarratives of pain and suffering as critical pedagogy: Disrupting oppression in educational contexts* (pp. 19–37). Routledge.

Dey, P., & Steyaert, C. (2016). Rethinking the space of ethics in social entrepreneurship: Power, subjectivity, and practices of freedom. *Journal of Business Ethics, 133*(4), 627–641.

Duarte Alonso, A., Kok, S., & O'Brien, S. (2020). "Profit is not a dirty word": Social entrepreneurship and community development. *Journal of Social Entrepreneurship, 11*(2), 111–133.

Farinha, L., Sebastião, J. R., Sampaio, C., & Lopes, J. (2020). Social innovation and social entrepreneurship: Discovering origins, exploring current and future trends. *International Review on Public and Nonprofit Marketing, 17*(1), 77–96.

Kester, G. H. (2011). *The one and the many: Contemporary collaborative art in a global context.* Duke University Press.

Kumari, R., Kwon, K-S., Lee, B-H., & Choi, K. (2020). Co-creation for social innovation in the ecosystem context: The role of higher educational institutions. *Sustainability, 12*(307), 1–21.

Kwong, J. (1993). Canadian universities in an age of austerity: Moving towards the business model. *Oxford Review of Education, 19*(1), 65–77.

Lawrence, E., Dunn, M.W., & Weislfeld-Spolter, S. (2018). Developing leadership potential in graduate students with assessment, self-awareness, reflection and coaching. *Journal of Management Development, 37*(8), 634–651.

Mathie, A. & Gaventa, J. (2015). Planting the seeds of a new economy: Learning from citizen-led innovation. In A. Mathie & J. Gaventa (Eds.), *Citizen-led innovation for a new economy* (pp. 1–23). Fernwood Publishing.

Mika, J.P., Warren, L., Foley, D., & Palmer, F.R. (2018). Perspectives on Indigenous entrepreneurship, innovation and enterprise. *Journal of Management & Organization, 23*(6), 767–773.

Milley, P., Szijarto, B., & Bennett, K. (2020). The landscape of social innovation in Canadian universities: An empirical analysis. *Canadian Journal of Nonprofit and Social Economy Research, 11*(1), 21–41.

Moffatt, K., Panitch, M., Parada, H., Todd, S., Barnoff, L., & Aslett, J. (2016). Essential cogs in the innovation machine: The discourse of innovation in Ontario educational reform. *Review of Education, Pedagogy and Cultural Studies, 38*(4), 317–340.

Moulaert, F., & MacCallum, D. (2019). *Advanced introduction to social innovation.* Edward Elgar Publishing.

Nandan, M., London, M., & Blum, T.C. (2014). Community practice social entrepreneurship: An interdisciplinary approach to graduate education. *International Journal of Social Entrepreneurship and Innovation, 3*(1), 51–70.

Nichols, A., Simon, J., & Gabriel, M. (2018). *New frontiers in social innovation research.* Palgrave Macmillan.

Nichols, N., Phipps, D., Provencal, J., & Hewitt, A. (2013). Knowledge mobilization, collaboration, and social innovation: Leveraging investments in higher education. *Canadian Journal of Nonprofit and Social Economy Research, 4*(1), 25–42.

Pel, B., Wittmayer, J. M., Avelino, F., Loorbach, D., & de Geus, T. (2023). How to account for the dark sides of social innovation? Transitions directionality in renewable energy prosumerism. *Environmental Innovation and Societal Transitions, 49*, 100775.

Rayner, C., & Bonnici, F. (2021). Complexity, scale, and depth. In C. Rayner & F. Bonnici (Eds.), *The systems work of social change: How to harness connection, context, and power to cultivate deep and enduring change* (pp. 18–32). Oxford University Press.

Rittel, H. W., & Webber, M. M. (1973). Dilemmas in a general theory of planning. *Policy Sciences, 4*(2), 155–169.

Slee, B., Burlando, C., Pisani, E., Secco, L., & Polman, N. (2021). Social innovation: A preliminary exploration of a contested concept. *Local Environment, 26*(7), 791–807.

Stauch, J. (2016). *Leadership for social innovation: Results of a pan-Canadian study on leadership learning for social change.* ISIRC Conference Proceedings, Glasgow.

Teasdale, S., Roy, M.J., Ziegler, R., Mauksch, S., Dey, P., & Raufflet, E.B. (2020). Everyone a changemaker? Exploring the moral underpinnings of social innovation discourse through real utopias. *Journal of Social Entrepreneurship, 12*(3), 417–437.

Thompson, N. (2012). *Living as form: Socially engaged art from 1991–2011.* MIT Press.

van der Have, R. P., & Rubalcaba, L. (2016). Social innovation research: An emerging area of innovation studies? *Research Policy, 45*(9), 1923–1935.

Wehbi, S., Panitch, M., Courneya, J., Fraticelli, R., Idrees, A., Machado, J., & Boonstra, O. (2023). (Re)Searching from within: Arriving at a scholarly approach to social innovation in higher education. *Educational Action Research, 31*(5), 920–930.

Social Innovation Re-Loaded

The Social as Innovation

Kiaras Gharabaghi

> **Learning Objectives**
> 1. Conceptualize social innovation as unfolding on a spectrum that focuses on the social at one end of the spectrum and on innovation at the other end.
> 2. Apply a critical lens on activities that are branded as social innovation but may be perpetuating existing social relations and power structures.
> 3. Construct new aesthetics of social innovation that de-centre business, economic and material outcomes and that re-centre social outcomes.

INNOVATION AND SOCIAL INNOVATION are not the same thing. Innovation can exist and unfold across many dimensions and generally aims to find new ways of bringing together knowledge, technologies, economic instruments and implementation sciences to generate greater productivity, efficiency and more profitable outcomes (Edler, 2019; Johnson, 2001; Lorenz, 2010; Schwanen, 2017). In some fields, such as medicine, innovation aims to operationalize new discoveries related to health and health care, which still involves a drive toward greater efficiencies and profitable outcomes, but it also generates stories of new cures, vaccines and health-care solutions for individuals (Beran, Hirsch, & Yudkin, 2019; Health Canada, 2015; Michelson, 2022). Innovation is neither good nor bad, although it turns out that a great deal of innovation benefits particular groups in society more so than others, and such benefactor groups are usually those that also hold dominant and even hegemonic positions of power and influence (Holly & Comedy, 2022; Sandra-Schillo & Robinson, 2017; Thapa, 2021).

The most innovative thing about social innovation is that it allows us to abandon the structure of our knowledge drawn from long-standing disciplines and professional activities to which we have far more loyalty than we are willing to admit. Chapter 7 provides a specific example of this staid knowledge and its practices by critically examining the discipline of chemistry. While many social innovation scholars are busy trying to narrow — and eventually define — what social innovation is, I prefer to do the opposite. I walk away from the need to know and articulate what it is and instead admire the concept as an aesthetic unto itself. Aesthetic here refers to both the nature of beauty and the appreciation or the experience of beauty. I am using the term to denote two things: first, the immediate sensation of being attracted to the concept of social innovation itself as something of beauty; and second, how social innovation enables us to imagine a scene for the future that can reflect our aspirations for social belonging, connectedness and meaning.

The phrase "social innovation" has enormous aesthetic appeal. "Innovation" invokes images of progress, positive change and discoveries while the word "social" constrains the word "innovation" by imposing upon it a collective conscience and a clear mandate for accountability. Furthermore, whereas "innovation" is aspirational and forward-looking, yet not perhaps immediately accessible to everyone, "social" is indeed accessible such that everyone can see themselves represented. Unlike other words and phrases denoting change, such as "revolution," "anti-oppressive practice" or "social movements," "social innovation" conjures none of the violent imagery of a revolution or of oppression, nor does it aesthetically represent change as physical movement per se. I see the phrase "social innovation" as denoting a moment in time that captures the fluidity of our ambitions and aspirations. Social innovation, not as a phrase but as a process, can translate the aesthetic or the beauty of the term into an aesthetic of contradiction and tension that can tantalize the engagement of our senses and sensibilities in a way unparalleled by other social actions.

Given that this is my starting point, it follows that I reject almost everything that is branded as social innovation. I do not reject the benefits or value of activities branded as social innovation, but I reject the incursion of stale activity that is embedded in existing and largely oppressive social relations into the healing spheres of social innovation as I understand it. Perhaps some examples would be helpful, and so let me provide a list of things that I reject as social innovations. Building a library in a poverty-ridden African village is not innovative, nor is building water wells to give easier access to drinking water to communities that otherwise would have to walk miles to get to a safe water source. Micro-credit and loan schemes are not innovative either; they are mechanisms of debt imbued with a venture capitalist mentality. Anti-racist and anti-oppressive practices on their own are not social innovations; these are the foundations of ever-growing industries that are carving out new markets in oppressive spaces.

16 INTERRUPTING INNOVATION

Decolonizing postsecondary education is not a social innovation, though I do give it credit as a rhetorical innovation that has legitimized the righteous status of settlers on stolen lands more than colonization itself.

This list of items that I reject as social innovations may at first appear as rather disparate. What does building a library have to do with decolonizing education? How do micro-credit schemes relate to anti-oppressive practices? The common element of all these items is the deeply held belief that social innovation ought to solve problems, correct wrongs and advance the quality of how we live life, individually and together. Innovation itself is unlikely to solve problems without creating new ones, and social innovation specifically is often undone by the problem-solving approach so deeply embedded in innovation rhetoric. The "social" in social innovation is, in fact, furthered by the problems we experience as part of our collective gatherings, our collective being and our collective becoming. Far from solving problems, we ought to relish in them and regain our humanity from them.

In this chapter, I want to accomplish three things: First, I want to discuss the role of social problems in the context of social innovation. Specifically, I frame social innovation as a way of being in relation to social problems instead of a method for solving such problems. Second, I want to separate the material context of social innovations from their sensory context. By this, I want to re-frame how we recognize and assess social innovation as distinct from measuring material outcomes. Third, I want to provide sustenance for those who dare to imagine the social as central and as a priority in the context of social innovation. I will do this by first exposing the fallacy of the social innovator as the character to whom to aspire. Then, I will focus on the importance of empowering the social as an innovation unto itself. I recognize that in putting forward these three aims, I will inevitably create tensions and contradictions in my own argument. This is very much intentional and serves a purpose, the nature of which I hope to illuminate in the concluding section.

THE BENEFITS OF SOCIAL PROBLEMS

It may not be obvious to think of social problems as beneficial. Real people living real lives often experience real suffering because of deeply entrenched social problems. There is nothing trivial about racism, a lack of housing or the alienation of newcomers to a country. Elder abuse, child sex trafficking, poverty and violence against women are real and of enormous consequence to those who experience them. On the other hand, the world has never known a time without social problems. The dynamics of power and inequity, of racism and poverty, and of violence and social alienation have been present for as long as history has been documented. At the same time, the interventions in these social problems have been less than impressive, at least if the measure of that is whether these problems have persisted over time. It turns out that interventions, regardless of how innovative they may appear, nevertheless unfold within existing structures of political economies and therefore are themselves complicit in the social problems they are trying to solve (Froud, Johal, Montgomerie, & Williams, 2010). As discussed in Chapter 1, and as Nicholls and Murdock (2012, p. 4) point out, "social innovation is never neutral, but always political and socially constructed." We have adopted a sequential logic in which we identify social problems and then work to solve them, initially at local and contained levels, and eventually at scale. This logic has been the driver of social innovation as a field of practice. We regularly celebrate this approach to social innovation either by narrating anecdotal evidence based on the stories of very few individuals or by highlighting the creativity and grit of the social innovators who make it their mission to make the world a better place (Kelly et al., 2022). This is the heart of the problem. At some point, we must pause and consider the possibility that solving social problems may not always be a meaningful approach. Let me provide some examples.

Although there are many child and youth service systems in Canada, ranging from schools to mental health services, developmental services, child welfare and more, there are still many young people living among us for whom none of these systems seems like a particularly good fit. These systems are often challenged by these young people because their fundamental goal is to render any one individual within those systems less visible. Young people who stand out because of their externalizing behaviours are often labelled as mismatched for the system to which they have been referred. These young people are often defined as young people with complex needs, where such needs consist of the intersection of developmental and regulatory "disorders," such as fetal alcohol spectrum disorder and autism spectrum disorder, and a wide range of mental health diagnoses (Lindsay & Hoffman, 2015). There is no system that is designed to care for these young people; instead, they are referred to many systems, usually only to be passed on to the next system. Most obviously, it is the child and youth mental health system that is supposed to engage with these young people and their families, but that system rejects its responsibility to do something because the young people are not labelled primarily as young people with mental health challenges. From there, they are passed on to the child welfare system, but that system claims that these are not young people in need of protection, and therefore child welfare is not the right place to respond to their challenges. The education system either expels them (citing the safety and the right to protection of the "normal" students) or segregates them into behavioural classrooms where the young people don't want to be, the teachers don't want to teach, and the support staff don't want their careers to get stuck. Other systems are often engaged, most notably the youth criminal justice system, especially if the young person is Black or Indigenous (Fante-Coleman & Jackson-Best, 2020; Fritsch, Monaghan, & Van der Meulen, 2022).

The child- and youth-serving systems challenged by these young people have forever been trying to find innovative solutions to this social problem. What to do with young people for whom no system can provide help, or at least not the kind of help that would allow these young people to become less visible in our normed systems of education, community and family? The answer so far has been the procurement of private, containment-focused services in the form of group homes. Public systems give large amounts of money to private, for-profit operators who then ensure that these young people are locked away in a "treatment" setting where they will remain contained and therefore "safe" (Edwards, Laylor, King, & Parada, 2023). In other words, the solution to this social problem is incarceration — even if we use the euphemistic language of treatment and biomedical intervention for these carceral and coercive practices (Braun et al., 2020).

I cite this example of young people with complex needs to make two points about social problems and why our first mistake often is trying to solve such problems. The first point is that the solutions we find to circumstances we label as problems are often worse than the problems themselves because they uphold a wide range of oppressive practices that are grounded in state and public violence. Second, this is an excellent example of how social problems are solved not socially but anti-socially: they resist social dynamics by individualizing, pathologizing and violently containing the challenge to the status quo, ultimately.

We might also consider homelessness as another example of a social problem that has become increasingly visible, especially in dense urban areas across North America. Homelessness has existed forever, and there has never been an urban area (even in the ancient cities of Persepolis, Constantinople, Athens and Rome) where every person residing in that space had a private and safe space to live. It has always been the case that some people live on the streets, wander between greenspaces in urban areas or utilize charitable shelters (often religious institutions) to spend the night (Atkins & Osborne,

2006). Most of the time, homelessness is not considered a social problem; it is considered an unfortunate life circumstance for individuals that ought to be addressed through emergency services and charity.

These days, homelessness has been articulated as a "social" problem because of its intersections with other challenges, most notably the opioid crisis raging across downtown cores of metropolises. There is also the mental health crisis that has connected the homeless, largely in reputation rather than action, to downtown crime and a lack of safety for the middle-class citizens engaged in consumption (Vitale, 2010). In other words, homelessness is now a social problem based on its aesthetic (how it appears) and its impact on citizens not facing this problem. Innovations in addressing homelessness centre around one singular concept: removing this aesthetic and thereby mitigating the impact on citizens. Social housing, supportive housing, shelters, transitional housing programs and many more popular frameworks for dealing with the homeless all have in common the idea that we can remove the homeless from the streets.

This approach to homelessness is itself rooted in a thoroughly eurocentric, fundamentally white, and deeply material concept of home. It assumes that home is synonymous with a material structure such as a house or a building, combined with private property and propriety values congruent with the modern capitalist structures around us. Gone from this conceptualization of home are the centuries of principally nomadic ways of living evidenced in most parts of the world. Also gone are postmodern and poststructuralist concepts of home that are associated with the sensory experiences of belonging and emotional roots (Börjesson & Söderqvist, 2020; Soaita, 2018; Wehbi, et al., 2016). With that, gone are the lived experiences of forced and voluntary migration that have come to define much of the twenty-first century so far. The problem of homelessness is therefore not about the everyday struggles experienced by those deemed homeless. Instead, homelessness is labelled as a violation of the modern material aesthetic that upholds normative structures in society. Innovations to solve this problem therefore require a focus on the restoration of that modern, material aesthetic.

The problem with removing aesthetic challenges to the well-to-do sensibilities of beauty is that the aesthetic remains intact but now becomes hidden. The city is beautified through the absence of the homeless, but the containers where they are stored maintain homelessness and associated challenges. The solution is only for those who did not face the problem in the first place. It is worthwhile to recall that in Toronto, for example, the homeless were the ones who engaged in innovation some twenty-five years ago; they invented a pop-up service in the form of squeegeeing, whereby they earned money from cleaning drivers' windshields when they were stopped at red lights. After much outcry, government stepped in and solved that problem by prohibiting this practice (Parnaby, 2003). The result, not surprisingly, has been a homeless population once again seeking to eke out a living through panhandling or various forms of (often highly innovative) trickery.

These examples show that our solutions to social problems are often quite absurd and sometimes make the problem worse. The examples also show that most of our solutions to social problems draw on the same latent power embedded in dominant social spheres — specifically, the power to remove, to incarcerate, to segregate, to exercise surveillance and to redraw the social aesthetic such that its ugliest elements disappear from sight but not from existence (Abdillahi, 2022; Vitale, 2010). Jessop, Moulaert, Hulgart and Hamdouch (2013) capture the tension between the pro-social rhetoric of social innovation and the stark reality of perpetuating existing power relations and structural inequities well. The authors argue that social innovation ultimately is a "struggle between forces pursuing radical social innovation oriented to social emancipation and those seeking to maintain an asymmetrically organized social order biased toward agencies of profit-making, efficient markets, and business-friendly social relations" (p. 112). How might we think differently using the framework of social innovation? And how might such different thinking result in different actions? I suggest that we begin by questioning the inherent truth of the sequence we have largely accepted as foundational: we identify a problem and then seek a solution. What if we rejected this sequence? What if we rejected the idea that young people with complex needs or homeless people are problems in need of solutions?

Most social problems we identify are not actually social problems; they are problems of unequal privilege resulting in neglect of social possibilities and an advancement of privileged group goals (McDonell, 2023). For example, is the problem of homelessness best identified through the aesthetic of the unhoused, which forces us to see and have sensory experiences around men, women and transgender people living on the streets, perhaps not having access to showers or laundered clothes? Or is this problem better identified through the aesthetic of opulence, which captures images of absurdity whereby a handful of families take up acres of space in an otherwise dense urban environment? Is the aesthetic of homelessness represented through the privatization of public spaces which are under constant surveillance and always subject to the threat of coercion against anyone using such spaces in unintended ways? Are gates, locks, barriers and locked spaces symptomatic of what we now call the homelessness crisis in urban centres? Are the intersections with the opiate and mental health crises really not an aesthetic of the normative restrictions imposed by the pathways of privilege (Earp, Skorburg, Everett, & Savulescu, 2019; Szott, 2023)?

All of these questions point to the possibility that what we define as social problems are actually moments, spaces and an aesthetic that are inconvenient to those not really affected by the social problem. The concept of a social problem is not universal. It is context-specific and generally describes pressures on social norms that are upheld by those who benefit from such norms. This insight then raises the question as to whether there are benefits to social problems and how such benefits might manifest.

One way we might think about social problems such as homelessness, racism, addictions or the quality of life of elders is to focus on the "social" of these problems. We can, for example, understand the quality of life of elders as the outcome of social structures and norms. The elder occupies a position of weakness and vulnerability in social structures built for performance and productivity, as well as in the context of norms that value efficiency and growth. These are not congruent with the contributions of elders to society. Instead, elders contribute through relational connections across generations and different social eras and through experiential knowledge and wisdom (Viscogliosi et al., 2020; Wiles & Jayasinha, 2013). Within the context of existing social structures and norms, they may be weak; however, within the context of strengthening the social connections across relationships, spaces and moments, they are essential, even if their contributions are largely unseen and often devalued (Ontario Human Rights Commission, 2021). It is this devaluing of their presence and the discounting of their role that sets the stage for abuse and neglect of quality of life. Many innovations perpetuate this process and help to set that stage by seeking to solve the problem through removal strategies.

A different way of thinking about social innovation, therefore, is to ask how not to remove the elderly from daily societal dynamics by placing them, for example, in institutional care facilities. Instead, we can ask how to re-centre the value of their contributions to the social context of communities. In so doing, we encounter a fundamental contradiction of social innovation as a phrase. The innovation component of the phrase suggests moving forward, advancing toward something new and improving on the past. A focus on the social, in contrast, suggests a move into the past in the storytelling of our elders. In other words, social innovation in this context is not at all a move forward nor a move toward solving a social problem. It is instead a re-visioning of that which already is there, but which finds new value in its connection and re-building of the social. When we focus on the social in social innovation, innovation is no longer about new things. Instead, the innovation is in the uncovering of that which has always been present but that had been cast aside in favour of innovation that eschewed the social; this latter kind of innovation is the root of social problems, not their solution.

The benefits of what we often label as a social problem, therefore, are found in the opportunity to rediscover what we already have. As Moulaert and Ailenei (2005, p. 2050) put it, the opportunity is "more like a reinter-pretation or reproduction of already lived social relations but within new contexts." This possibility, however, is only meaningful if we focus on the social in social innovation and aim to constantly reinforce the structures and norms of the social in our communities. One way to do that is to create space for stories; other ways is to include music, performance arts, visual arts, public gatherings, protest movements and solidarity movements, all of which enhance our appreciation of the social (Alkoby, Gharabaghi, & Panitch, 2023). Gibson-Graham and Roelvink (2013, p. 455) describe social innovation as "projects [that are] projects of inclusion, whether geared to-ward meeting the material needs of the marginalized, opening social arenas to the previously excluded, or giving 'voice' to those who have had little or no say in political life." With this framing in mind, when we encounter the homeless, the question ought not to be: How do we solve this problem? The question ought to be: What are we missing? And further: What social opportunity lies beneath our encounter with those whose lives unfold unhoused? What can we uncover about solidarity in tent cities emerging across major metropolises everywhere, even if parallel to such solidarity we also find violence? And how have our rigid and highly exclusive norma-tive concepts of mental health and well-being, or of addictions, reinforced homelessness as a social problem?

THE SENSORY CONTEXT OF SOCIAL INNOVATION

If one were to identify one singular idea that has captured our attention so far in the twenty-first century, it surely is the idea of trauma. Although trauma itself is nothing new, the ubiquity of the trauma narrative that sur-rounds us is extraordinary and likely fuelled by the latest discoveries in the brain sciences and neuro-scientific research (Van der Kolk, 2015). Across disciplines, trauma has been integrated into how we understand others and ourselves. Almost everyone is impacted by trauma. Black communities suffer from racial trauma. Indigenous communities suffer from intergenerational trauma. Victims of violence, physical or sexual abuse, and other forms of individualized, adverse experiences, suffer from trauma that has impacted the architecture of their brains. Along with the experience of trauma, we have identified the perpetrators of trauma as potentially anyone, any group, any setting and any context. Academic departments can be traumatizing because of oppressive practices. Anxiety resulting from an uncertain world can be traumatizing and debilitating for some (or for many). War, torture, migration, immigration, settlement, poverty, alienation, loneliness, divorce, ineffective parenting, witnessing violence, being subjected to the possibility of something terrible, flight delays, lost baggage, the fear of missing out on something (FOMO), offensive rhetoric on social media — virtually anything can set off a chain of trauma, trauma-victimhood and trauma-informed responses.

The concept of trauma is certainly real. The brain sciences demonstrating changes to the architecture of the brain are real too (Peverill et al., 2023; Van der Kolk, 2015, 2016). What is not real is the idea that trauma is a change, something new or a social problem in need of a response. Indeed, it is not entirely clear whether the concept of trauma adds anything to how we exist in the world and in relation to one another. What would be different if we simply did not talk about trauma at all, did not label trauma and refused to give a name to the way we are with one another? The question is partly rhetorical but also very real. In fact, institutional refusals to label and name trauma have caused a great deal of harm. For example, soldiers and first responders experiencing trauma in the exercise of their daily duties, and later experiencing significant challenges in their post-professional lives, have largely been abandoned by their institutional (state) employers and left to their own devices. The refusal to recognize trauma, and therefore to offer support to those impacted, has caused enormous harm (including homicide and suicide) to individuals, families and even entire communities (Russell, Schaubel, & Figley, 2018). We can make similar observations about children being separated from their asylum-seeking parents who are often held in custody (Mares, 2021); women being invalidated in their reporting of sexual violence (Webermann & Holland, 2022); or Indigenous women and girls being abducted, violated and murdered across Canada, and likely across the United States, Australia, and Central and South America (Ficklin et al., 2022).

Labelling and naming trauma would seem important to ensure that individuals impacted gain access to supports and interventions. It would also seem important in the context of policy and government investment to combat the much larger community effects of trauma, as is necessary in the example of MMIWG2S+. And yet, we see only one aspect of the trauma problem being addressed, while the other continues to be sidestepped, avoided, denied or contested. Specifically, we can see the innovation machines within pharmaceutical companies and among prestige professionals, such as psychiatrists, working hard to own the narrative of trauma treatment and trauma-informed practices, introducing them as health-care strategies and individualized solutions for those impacted (Callaghan, 2019). On the other hand, outside of Indigenous communities, we see nothing on the community front; Indigenous women, girls and 2SLGBTQI+ continue to go missing and be murdered, with policy responses to innovate change either intentionally sidestepped or altogether anything but innovative (McDiarmid, 2019). One way of understanding this issue is to recognize that when we talk about innovation in a social context (spoken as "social innovation"), we are talking about individualization and furthering the abdication of our faith in the social. Montgomery (2016, p. 1985) makes this point forcefully, noting that the term "social" is "frequently couched in terms which privilege market competition, with the 'social' repositioned within a commodified frame and an emphasis on 'supply and demand' as well as the potential for increased efficiency and savings that can be made to public finances."

Social innovation, as I am constructing it, is surprisingly relevant to the issue of trauma. Its applicability is not obvious because it does not pertain to solving the trauma, nor does it lend itself to any material approaches to generating "success stories" and narratives of productivity despite the trauma. Instead, a social innovation approach to trauma requires us to abandon problem-solving approaches and the problem-solution sequence of innovation narratives in favour of narratives that centre the social. This is not merely a philosophical or ethical proposition, but an evidence-based proposition drawing on literature. Social engagement, often in the form of performance arts or land-based practices, produces impacts that are transformative to those who identify trauma or traumatic events as core elements of the way they are in the world (Gallimore & Herndon, 2019; Helmick, 2023). Trauma-informed practice, in this context, does not mean trauma-informed cognitive behaviour therapies, dialectical behavioural therapies or pharmacological approaches to dulling the senses. It means quite the contrary: rediscovering the social context of our humanity in relation to nature, land, spirituality and social engagement (Redvers, 2020).

As a sensory experience, social innovation produces contexts of being with one another and the world around us that connect us to spaces and moments of feeling (and hearing, sensing, seeing) one another through body movement, spoken word, verse, prose, music and a spontaneity of interactions in groups. Of direct relevance to this discussion, Chapter 3 offers examples of the use of socially engaged art practices to address "social problems" in ways that create connection and belonging. Social innovation creates media for belonging, expression and feeling alive; it transforms suspicions of trauma into new ways of greeting the world around us.

There are, in fact, many examples of social innovation initiatives in relation to the trauma problem (see Brend et al., 2020; Rogers & White, 2017; Streater, 2022; Randall, Chan, & Burker, 2021). Such initiatives are almost always local, highly targeted at specific groups and virtually never taken to scale, as this would require a level of funding and support from broader and largely public bodies. Still, we can see dance, theatre, visual arts and music interventions for youth impacted by racial trauma (Streater, 2022), for Indigenous youth dealing with intergenerational trauma and identity vacuums (France, 2020) and for refugees dealing with trauma associated with the experiences of war, migration and settlement (Baker, 2006).

I use the example of trauma to pull social innovation away from the material context in which it often finds expression, exemplified by consumption, outcome-based approaches to change and charitable models of supporting marginalized communities. Instead, I bring social innovation firmly into the realm of the sensory, embodied in activities designed to rediscover, and to reinforce, the social. The innovative part of social innovation lies in the social as it is experienced through our senses, be that through togetherness, interest in one another's ways of being in the world or through our connections to land and nature that hold us in community in the first place.

The sensory context of social innovation aims to transform not our productivity nor our material well-being, but instead, how we are in relation to others and our relationship to the world around us. I refer to it as a sensory context because it articulates social innovation as activities that centre ways of being, ways of seeing and ways of feeling to produce something analogous to what was long ago called the "sociological imagination" (Mills, 1959). Building on the political resistance embedded in the original concept of the sociological imagination, the sensory context of social innovation aims to disrupt the status quo. Social innovation makes life better for communities in its resistance to this material narrative of change, which has, for decades, increased inequities and obscured community identity and desires. The innovation in social innovation is thus to be found in both the celebration and the melancholy embedded in the social gathering, the social connection and the social aesthetic.

THE FALLACY OF THE SOCIAL INNOVATOR

How does social innovation happen? Who makes it happen? Can social innovation happen in the absence of a social innovator? The answers to these kinds of questions are quite different depending on one's way of understanding social innovation. Social innovation is real; social innovators are not — at least if we understand social innovation outside of its material and solution-focused frame. Yet it has become quite common to identify changemakers and celebrate them as social innovators. Muhammad Yunus, founder of the Grameen Bank in Bangladesh, for example, has been celebrated as a social innovator on the strengths of operationalizing microcredit to enable marginalized people, and notably women, to start businesses (Turvey & Kong, 2006). Similarly, Bill Drayton, founder of Ashoka, has been held up as a social innovator on account of starting Ashoka as a not-for-profit organization based in the US that pairs **social entrepreneurs** with social problems around the world and aims to promote change-making among emerging talent (Sen, 2007). Blake Mycoskie, founder of TOMS, is identified as a social innovator on the strength of founding a shoe business (which now has many more products) that donates a percentage of sales to various charitable activities (Talpalaru, 2014).

The terms social innovator and social entrepreneur are often used interchangeably, which demonstrates the enormous focus on addressing social problems (without clarity on who declares things to constitute a social problem) through business solutions that create sustainable funding mechanisms for what essentially boils down to charity. Valorization of the "individual" is entirely incongruent with social innovation as an aesthetic of the "social." Instead, this valorization puts forward the rugged determination and the perceived extraordinary sacrifice/courage/heroic altruism of an individual as the brand for the innovation. "The trope of the heroic entrepreneur being espoused by the technocratic school should not surprise us given their neoliberal inspiration" (Montgomery, 2016, p. 1986).

As part of this process, social innovation deteriorates into a series of awards and accolades for the changemaker, obscuring the real lives lived by those for whom change was enacted. Furthermore, it requires the victimization of those the social innovation is intended to address. Building water wells using a creative entrepreneurial strategy in remote African villages is only useful if we construct the African villager as helpless and needy, and remove from the African villager any value associated with local traditions, knowledges, ways of being and sensory sensations of everyday life. Instead, it is the technical knowledge and the will to make a difference on the part of the innovator that will improve the lives of the otherwise unknown and largely anonymous people. "Social innovation holds the key to our social ills. Social entrepreneurs are the people most able to deliver that innovation" (Leadbeater, 1997, p. 20). Furthermore, as Montgomery (2016) argues, the push for technocratic knowledge at the heart of social innovation to lead the charge in solving problems in marginalized communities is at the same time a push to depoliticize inequity and social injustice, thus demobilizing any resistance to it.

A story that was told to me some time ago illustrates the point. A social innovator noticed on a visit to an African village that the women in the village had to travel a considerable distance to retrieve potable water, taking hours out of their day and leaving them unavailable for other activities, including supervising their children or engaging in productive, income-generating activities. The innovator assembled a team of experts, and using creative innovations, they managed to build a water well right in the village so that women no longer had to travel to get potable water. All seemed fine and the problem of a lack of access to potable water appeared to have been solved. About ten years later, a group of researchers were in that same village. When they asked the local elders about social problems in the village, the elders spoke of an enormous increase in family violence, specifically violence against women in the village. This violence, they said, started to happen about ten years ago and had intensified ever since. The researcher started talking with the women of the village to try to understand why such violence started emerging ten years ago and appeared to be worsening. What they found was that after the well had been built in the village, the women no longer travelled together as a group each day to fetch water. As a result, they lost their connections with one another, spent more time in isolation in their homes and lost their collective power in the context of family and kinship dynamics. It turns out that the hours spent travelling each day were critically important in strengthening the women's collective capacity to keep their men in line. They talked with each other, alerted each other to potential problems in families and took care of each other through their tight social network. Once the well was built and the travel became unnecessary, the network fell apart and the social dynamics of the village changed dramatically.

Some version of this story, as it turns out, is a frequently told parable

28 INTERRUPTING INNOVATION

among people involved in international development work and globally focused community development work. It has many similarities to, and may even have been influenced in its nuance by, a real, social innovation called the "PlayPump" that originated in southern Africa. This initiative was originally hailed as a brilliant intervention in the challenge of access to clean water but it has since been viewed critically after encountering a range of problems. (For the original social innovation, see *National Geographic*, n.d.; for the critiques of it that have emerged, see Borland, 2011; and *PBS News*, 2018.)

This story speaks to the concerns associated with identifying social problems in the first place (in this case, the wrong identification of the lack of access to nearby potable water as being a social problem), but it also speaks to the fallacy of the individual innovator. From the perspective of that innovator, access to potable water in the village was an assumed requirement for building capacity for the villagers. This assumption may well be congruent with the innovator's lived experiences. As it turns out, however, it is an assumption that is inherently anti-social when it is acted upon based entirely on the innovator's determination to make a difference. This innovation, in fact, destroyed the social by eliminating an ongoing and existing social innovation that had emerged from the women's ways of being together. Their use of the travelling time to fetch water as a way of maintaining a social network that governed the village's social dynamics, including its family dynamics, *was* the social innovation. In the material and neoliberal narrative of social innovation (and entrepreneurship) as an emerging field of practice, a group of women as a social network does not lend itself to valorization. The field requires the character of the innovator to anchor itself. Yet, it is precisely the women and their knowledge and connections, using walking and talking time as a form of social design, who are the innovators because they are designing a fluid aesthetic of the social.

Social innovation as a way of celebrating the social cannot be furthered through the greatness of one. Instead, social innovation necessarily relies on the convergence of the ideas and ways of being of many who come together across similarities and differences to generate collective spaces and moments in time. People find opportunities that can include healing from trauma, building strengths, forming new connections and creating belonging and inclusiveness for all. As a process, social innovation is inherently anti-hierarchy and anti-individual leadership, because any hierarchy and any individually driven leadership inherently fragment the social. It is no longer *the* social; it becomes someone's version, or narrative, of *a* social. To this end, Montgomery (2016, p. 1991) describes how a more democratically oriented version of social innovation offers "a rejection of such hierarchical figureheads or elites, sometimes engraving this rejection into the very names of their organisations such as Fabrica Sin Patron, an exemplar of the recuperated workplace movement in Argentina or through the exclamations of activists in New York's Zuccotti Park [during the Occupy Wall Street Movement] that 'we are the 99 %.'"

It is worthwhile to defend the defence of the social. Throughout this chapter, I have argued that social innovation often is anti-social in its orientation and serves to fragment a social aesthetic and replace it with the heroic imagery of the innovator and the promise of resolving chronic social problems. The aesthetic we now confront is one of profound individualism in which growth and productivity are driven by individuals and measured by their impact on the lives of individuals *as* individuals. Montgomery (2016, p. 1988) argues that within this neoliberal approach to social innovation, "the realm of the social becomes absorbed into the paradigm of competition." I am not suggesting that current innovation strategies across disciplines and fields of practice are misguided, wrong or harmful, although there are instances where they are. I am, however, suggesting that social innovation as an emerging field is at significant risk of being little more than a novel mechanism by which we perpetuate the very structures and processes that generate the social problems we now aim to solve innovatively. If this is where social innovation is headed, there will be little value added and much of the rhetoric of social innovation will remain just that, entirely congruent with the structural and systemic dynamics of neoliberal political economies.

The "social" in social innovation must be our central preoccupation. Social problems, regardless of how we define these or whose narrative we centre, are problems because of the fragmentation, and indeed the destruction, of the social aesthetic. We measure growth and development through indicators of material growth and productivity. This, I argue, is misguided. Social innovation ought to produce an image of the future that demonstrates value in gathering, in all our relations (Talaga, 2018), in the spirit of *ubuntu* (Samuel, 2023), in relational network building and in generating moments where communities of sameness and differences find belonging and desire. The social in social innovation is not about solving social problems; it is about learning to be together, connected in a complicated world that features enormous inequities and moments of inhumanity. The social is what protects us from such inhumanities. The innovation is the promotion of the social in a world aiming to destroy it.

30 INTERRUPTING INNOVATION

CONCLUSION: RE-LOADING SOCIAL INNOVATION

Social innovation is not about the specific events, projects or activities we undertake in the name of growth, development or progress. And it is not about solving social problems, at least not in any concrete measure. It is instead a way of being in the world that centres social connection and networks as the foundation for moving toward social justice. As noted in Chapter 1, the connection between social innovation and social justice has always been tenuous and somewhat indeterminate, although Moulaert and Ailenei (2005, p. 2037) argue that "social innovation [...] is mainly about the (re) introduction of social justice into production and allocation systems." This relationship becomes much clearer when we understand social innovation as a celebration of the social rather than a valorization of innovation. Within this framework of social innovation, where the social *is* the innovation, we move away from social innovation as political economy layered within the broader, neoliberal world order. We move toward social innovation as an aspiration for a social aesthetic that is inclusive and produces a sensory context of belonging, sharing and common aspirations for change.

I have intentionally focused on a limited number of themes within the broader discussions about social innovation as an evolving field of practice and an intellectual and interdisciplinary field of study. Clearly, the rich and ever-expanding literature on social innovations suggests that there are many more themes and topics, and certainly many examples of social innovation activities, that could be discussed, analyzed, critically engaged and ultimately further developed. Indeed, the following chapters in this book will provide additional perspectives and thematic foci. I chose to focus on three relatively central concerns: 1) the idea that social innovation is about finding solutions to social problems; 2) the concept of a sensory approach to social innovation as an alternative to the more dominant material approach; and 3) the critique of the social innovator narrative, combined with a defence of the social, as something worthy of defence.

I want to reiterate that social innovation offers opportunities to be and think differently. As an academic field and a professional practice, it offers transformative epistemologies and methodologies through its disregard of traditional disciplinary silos and its embrace of knowledge emanating from the social. Much has been said in the literature about the measure of social innovation being not about outcomes but social impact. The discussion has tried to support the case for social impact by prioritizing the generative movements toward the social. What does this mean concretely? Well, it means a dance, theatre or performance gathering for refugee women facing the struggles of settling in a new and alien environment is a social innovation. It is that not because an innovator determined it to be that; it is a social innovation because the complex interface of body movement, interpersonal relationships and collective sense of purpose and being generate a new social aesthetic in which otherwise often disoriented and alienated women can sense their belonging.

It also means that creative and undoubtedly useful initiatives such as food distribution networks, supportive housing, school breakfast programs, social enterprises and others are not *inherently* social innovations, although that does not mean that these are not desirable activities. Although innovative to the extent that they aim to solve or mitigate social problems, they are always at risk of doing so by celebrating the solution and the innovator driving that solution at the expense of generating new social aesthetics that allow people to re-vision life itself. Such initiatives can exist at the threshold of social innovation, but they cannot become social innovations without centring the social. Even if the outcomes of a breakfast program may increase the percentage of young people ready to learn in school with full tummies, it leaves the children, their parents and the teachers exactly where they were before breakfast — waiting for the next day to carry the same requirement of charity and extra effort to ensure kids are fed in the morning. The social impact of these initiatives is difficult to ascertain precisely because these initiatives prioritize the specific outcome over the generation of new ways of being together that can be felt and absorbed and therefore serve to offer new possibilities for tomorrow.

Reflection Questions

1. What seemingly mundane activities do many people engage in regularly by themselves that could usefully serve as foundations for creating new spaces for the social?

2. Sometimes good things happen that improve life for many people, often entire communities. Why does it often seem important or necessary to credit such good things to an individual, or a small group of individuals, as the creators of such good things? Why do good things have to be associated with someone exercising their individual agency?

3. I repeatedly refer to charity as something other than social innovation. But can charity also be a social innovation? Are these two phrases necessarily mutually exclusive? Why or why not?

REFERENCES

Abdillahi, I. (2022). *Black women under state: Surveillance, poverty, & violence of social assistance*. ARP Books.

Alkoby, A., Gharabaghi, K., & Panitch, M. (2023). *Social innovation for social justice*. Toronto Metropolitan University Press.

Atkins, E. M., & Osborne, R. (2006). *Poverty in the Roman world*. Cambridge University Press.

Baker, B. A. (2006). Art speaks in healing survivors of war: The use of art therapy in treating trauma survivors. *Journal of Aggression, Maltreatment & Trauma, 12*(1-2), 183–198.

Beran, D., Hirsch, I. B., & Yudkin, J. S. (2019). What is innovation in the area of medicines? The example of insulin and diabetes. *Diabetic Medicine, 36*(12), 1526.

Börjesson, U., & Söderqvist Forkby, Å. (2020). The concept of home: unaccompanied youths' voices and experiences. *European Journal of Social Work, 23*(3), 475–485.

Borland, R. (2011). *Surface tension: The problem with the PlayPump*. [Video]. YouTube. youtube.com/watch?v=e1Empo4dscA

Braun, M. T., Adams, N. B., O'Grady, C. E., Miller, D. L., & Bystrynski, J. (2020). An exploration of youth physically restrained in mental health residential treatment centers. *Children and Youth Services Review, 110*, 104826.

Brend, D., Fréchette, N., Milord-Nadon, A., Harbinson, T., & Colin-Vezina, D. (2020). Implementing trauma-informed care through social innovation in residential care facilities serving elementary school children. *International Journal of Child and Adolescent Resilience, 7*(1), 222–232.

Callaghan, C. W. (2019). Critical perspectives on international pharmaceutical innovation: Malthus, Foucault and resistance. *Critical Perspectives on International Business, 15*(1), 68–86.

Earp, B. D., Skorburg, J. A., Everett, J. A. C., & Savulescu, J. (2019). Addiction, Identity, Morality. *AJOB Empirical Bioethics, 10*(2), 136–153.

Edler, J. (2019). A costly gap: The neglect of the demand side in Canadian innovation policy. *IRPP Insight, 28*. Institute for Research on Public Policy.

Edwards, T., Laylor, A., King, B., & Parada, H. (2023). When home reminds me of jail: The carceral nature of out-of-home care for Black youth in Ontario's child welfare system. *Children and Youth Services Review, 155*, 107309.

Fante-Coleman, T., & Jackson-Best, F. (2020). Barriers and facilitators to accessing mental healthcare in Canada for Black youth: A scoping review. *Adolescent Research Review, 5*(2), 115–136.

Ficklin, E., Tehee, M., Killgore, R. M., Isaacs, D., Mack, S., & Ellington, T. (2022). Fighting for our sisters: Community advocacy and action for missing and murdered Indigenous women and girls. *Journal of Social Issues, 78*(1), 53–78.

France, H. (2020). Creative arts and the Indigenous Healing Circle within an Indigenous context. *Canadian Journal of Counselling and Psychotherapy, 54*(3), 413.

Fritsch, K., Monaghan, J., & Van der Meulen, E. (2022). *Disability injustice: Confronting criminalization in Canada*. University of British Columbia Press.

Froud, J., Johal, S., Montgomerie, J., & Williams, K. (2010). Escaping the tyranny of earned income? The failure of finance as social innovation. *New Political Economy, 15*(1), 147–164.

Gallimore, R. B., & Herndon, G. (2019). *Art from trauma: Genocide and healing beyond Rwanda*. University of Nebraska Press.

Gibson-Graham, J. K., & Roelvink, G. (2013). Social innovation for community economies: How action research creates "other worlds." In F. Moulaert, D. MacCallum, A. Mehmood, & A. Hamdouch (Eds.), *The international handbook on social innovation: Collective action, social learning and transdisciplinary research* (pp. 466–480). Edward Elgar Publishing.

Health Canada. (2015). *Unleashing innovation: Excellent health care for Canada. Report of the Advisory Panel on Health Innovation.* Government of Canada. www.healthycanadians.gc.ca/publications/health-system-systeme-sante/report-healthcare-innovation-rapport-soins/alt/report-healthcare-innovation-rapport-soins-eng.pdf

Helmick, L. (2023). Expressing trauma through therapeutic art-based trauma-informed practice with/in a collective happening. *Studies in Art Education, 64*(3), 324–343.

Holly, J., & Comedy, Y. L. (2022). Whitey on the moon: Racism's maintenance of inequity in invention and innovation. *Technology and Innovation, 22*(3), 331–340.

Jessop, B., Moulaert, F., Hulgard, L., & Hamdouch, A. (2013). Social innovation research: A new stage in innovation analysis? In F. Moulaert, D. MacCallum, A. Mehmood, & A. Hamdouch (Eds.), *The international handbook on social innovation: Collective action, social learning and transdisciplinary research* (pp. 110–130). Edward Elgar Publishing.

Johnson, D. (2001). What is innovation and entrepreneurship? Lessons for larger organisations. *Industrial and Commercial Training, 33*(4), 135–140.

Kelly, L., Perkins, V., Zuraik, A., & Luse, W. (2022). Social impact: The role of authentic leadership, compassion and grit in social entrepreneurship. *The Journal of Entrepreneurship, 31*(2), 298–329.

Leadbeater, C. (1997). *The rise of the social entrepreneur.* Demos.

Lindsay, S., & Hoffman, A. (2015). A complex transition: lessons learned as three young adults with complex care needs transition from an inpatient paediatric hospital to adult community residences. *Child Care, Health & Development, 41*(3), 397–407.

Lorenz, R. (2010). What is innovation? Insights and perspectives on the term "innovation." *International Journal of Technology Intelligence and Planning, 6*(1), 63–75.

Mares, S. (2021). Mental health consequences of detaining children and families who seek asylum: A scoping review. *European Child & Adolescent Psychiatry, 30*(10), 1615–1639.

McDiarmid, J. (2019). *Highway of Tears: A true story of racism, indifference and the pursuit of justice for missing and murdered Indigenous women and girls.* Doubleday Canada.

McDonell, N. (2023). *Quiet street: On American privilege.* Pantheon Books.

Michelson, G. K. (2022). Accelerating the pace of innovation for the greater good. *Technology and Innovation, 22*(2), 153–156.

Mills, C. W. (1959). *Sociological imagination.* Oxford University Press.

Montgomery, T. (2016). Are social innovation paradigms incommensurable? *Voluntas, 27*(4), 1979–2000.

Moulaert, F., & Ailenei, O. (2005). Social economy, third sector and solidarity relations: A conceptual synthesis from history to present. *Urban Studies, 42*(11), 2037–2053.

National Geographic (2008, January 9,). *Playpumps International.* [Video]. YouTube. *youtube.com/watch?v=qjgcHOWcWGE*

Nicholls, A., & Murdock, A. (2012). The nature of social innovation. In A. Nicholls & A. Murdock (Eds.), *Social innovation: Blurring boundaries to reconfigure markets* (pp. 1–30). Palgrave Macmillan.

Ontario Human Rights Commission (2021). *Time for action: Advancing human rights for older Ontarians.* Ontario Human Rights Commission. ohrc.on.ca/sites/default/files/attachments/Time_for_action%3A_Advancing_human_rights_for_older_Ontarians.pdf

Parnaby, P. (2003). Disaster through dirty windshields law, order and Toronto's squeegee kids. *Canadian Journal of Sociology, 28*(3), 281–307.

PBS News (2018). *Frontline World: Troubled Waters takes a second look at PlayPumps.* [Video]. YouTube. youtube.com/watch?v=PTJgAK7e9ro

Peverill, M., Rosen, M. L., Lurie, L. A., Sambrook, K. A., Sheridan, M. A., & McLaughlin, K. A. (2023). Childhood trauma and brain structure in children and adolescents. *Developmental Cognitive Neuroscience, 59*, 101180.

Randall Emmons, A. E., Chan, D. V., & Burker, E. J. (2021). Yoga therapy as an innovative treatment for complex trauma. *Journal of Applied Rehabilitation Counseling, 52*(4), 266–281.

Redvers, J. (2020). "The land is a healer": Perspectives on land-based healing from Indigenous practitioners in Northern Canada. *International Journal of Indigenous Health, 15*(1), 90–107.

Russell, M. C., Schaubel, S. R., & Figley, C. R. (2018). The darker side of military mental healthcare part two: Five harmful strategies to manage its mental health dilemma. *Psychological Injury and Law, 11*(1), 37–68.

Samuel, O. S. (2023). Practicing Ubuntu. *The Philosophical Forum, 54*(3), 143–159.

Sandra-Schillo, R., & Robinson, R. (2017). Inclusive innovation in developed countries: The who, what, why, and how. *Technology Innovation Management Review, 7*(7), 34–46.

Schwanen, D. (2017). Innovation policy in Canada: A holistic approach. *C.D. Howe Institute Commentary, 497.*

Sen, P. (2007). Ashoka's Big Idea: Transforming the world through social entrepreneurship. *Futures: The Journal of Policy, Planning and Futures Studies, 39*(5), 534–553.

Soaita, A. M. (2018). Reimagining home in the 21st century. *Housing Studies, 33*(2), 337–338.

Streater, O. K. N. (2022). Truth, justice and bodily accountability: Dance movement therapy as an innovative trauma treatment modality. *Body, Movement and Dance in Psychotherapy, 17*(1), 34–53.

Talaga, T. (2018). *All our relations: Finding the path forward.* House of Anansi Press.

Talpalaru, M. (2014). Blake Mycoskie, TOMS, and life narratives of conspicuous giving. *Biography, 37*(1), 168–190.

Thapa, N. (2021). Forms of exclusion in the innovation process: An analysis of access to formal organizations by small plantation growers in India. *Innovation and Development,* (forthcoming), 1–19.

Turvey, C. G., & Kong, R. (2006). Biography: Dr. Muhammad Yunus, founder of the Grameen Bank and 2006 Nobel Peace Prize recipient. *Agricultural Finance Review, 66*(2), 137–143.

Unger, R.M. (2015). The task of the social innovation movement. In A. Nicholls, J. Simon, & M. Gabriel (Eds.), *New frontiers in social innovation research* (pp. 2–13). Palgrave Macmillan.

Van der Kolk, B. A. (2015). *The body keeps the score: Brain, mind, and body in the healing of trauma.* Penguin Books.

Viscogliosi, C., Asselin, H., Basile, S., Borwick, K., Couturier, Y., Drolet, M.-J., Gagnon, D., Obradovic, N., Torrie, J., Zhou, D., & Levasseur, M. (2020). Importance of Indigenous elders' contributions to individual and community wellness: Results from a scoping review on social participation and intergenerational solidarity. *Canadian Journal of Public Health, 111*(5), 667–681.

Vitale, A. S. (2010). The Safer Cities Initiative and the removal of the homeless: Reducing crime or promoting gentrification on Los Angeles' Skid Row? *Criminology & Public Policy, 9*(4), 867–873.

Webermann, A. R., & Holland, K. J. (2022). Inconsistency is the consistency: The Title IX reporting process for sexual and gender-based misconduct within Maryland public universities. *Psychology of Women Quarterly, 46*(4), 468–483.

Wehbi, S., Parada, H., George, P., & Lessa, I. (2016). Going home: Social work across and about borders. *International Social Work, 59*(2), 284–292.

Wiles, J. L., & Jayasinha, R. (2013). Care for place: The contributions older people make to their communities. *Journal of Aging Studies, 27*(2), 93–101.

Pro-Tests and *Making with Place*

Socially Engaged Arts Activisms
and Innovations reCentring the Margins

Phyllis Novak and Charlotte Lombardo

> **Learning Objectives**
> 1. To understand and theorize socially engaged arts as social innovation for movement-making.
> 2. To illustrate how socially engaged arts are mobilized by equity-seeking young people to reCentre the margins, drawing on artworks and learnings from the *Making with Place* project.

COMMUNITIES ON THE MARGINS have been at the forefront of social justice struggles for centuries. bell hooks (1984, p. ii) reminds us that they have a unique duality of vision needed for action while living on the "edge": "We developed a particular way of seeing reality […] unknown to most of our oppressors, that sustained us, aided us in our struggle to transcend poverty and despair, [and] strengthened our sense of self and our solidarity." This vantage from a socially constructed "outside" that is the "margins" involves reflecting the impacts of a dominant centre back to itself while at the same time intuiting, inspiring and activating liberatory ways forward, beyond that centre with its limitations and its exclusions. The projects discussed here illuminate the generative power of **socially engaged arts** by young people, making on the margins to inspire and lead social innovation focused on a world-building where no one is left behind. Through these projects, socially engaged arts emerge as practice-movement spaces for young artists to build collective capacity, movement-mindedness and action.

To move through these contemplations, we situate the discussion within the scholarship on socially engaged arts that looks at how they can play an integral role in building activism, particularly by those on the margins. We illustrate learning drawn from research-creation collaborations with young artists through a local initiative called *Making with Place*, driven by social-movement characteristics. We do so in order to dive into the possibilities that exist in thinking of socially engaged arts as a practice (for) movement generated in and by community that is for developing collective care, identity and action toward radical belonging. At the time, Phyllis Novak was the artistic director and coordinator of the project and one of its lead researchers; and Charlotte Lombardo engaged with Novak and the *Making with Place* artists in participatory research exploring co-theorizations of change that emerged from the research creations. Both were able to focus on graduate students through this project as it evolved from research to community-designed socially engaged public art. The initiative partnered with the community arts organization, SKETCH Working Arts, of which Novak is the founding director.

SOCIALLY ENGAGED ARTS AND SOCIAL MOVEMENTS — WHAT MAKES THEM SO SIGNIFICANT IN PROPELLING CHANGE?

Socially engaged arts (SEA) is dynamic, collaborative social innovation in artmaking. It includes interaction, reflection and dialogue, through which participants can make sense of their current situations, explore critical issues that matter to them and creatively express and experiment with collective ways to move forward. *Making with Place* began as a three-year research-creation initiative in SEA, through which a series of public artworks evolved to become part of Toronto's Year of Public Art (2020–22). In the works, young people navigating the "margins" explored their desires and intentions for community, culture and place. At the core of the project were ethical relations with self, land and community that remapped and dismantled boxed colonial or capitalist geographies, and that activated processes and practices in collective care and regenerative reciprocity. *Making with Place* demonstrated durational SEA to create **practice movements** resulting in relational becoming and radical belonging (Goeman, 2013; Lombardo et al., 2023).

SEA can be powerful across the spectrum of social movement action: in developing movement framing or ideology; in sustaining participation; and in communicating and diffusing issues, goals and action among communities. Castellano (2021) emphasizes that SEA is much more than a trend or artistic discipline that broadens the role of art in society as emancipatory praxis needed for movement action. He claims that, as a praxis, SEA intersects across many disciplines as a mode of "doing" culture and as "a powerful tool for despecializing, undisciplining and unmastering cultural interactions" (p. 7). This dual activity of doing and undoing through collaborative engagement and interaction makes SEA a powerful process to incubate and experiment with movement praxis. It engages those involved to build a collective voice, identity and solidarity so as to confront and break down hegemonic power and singularity. Castellano calls SEA a "culturally mediated space of practice and thought" (2021, p. 59), in which the doing and undoing are unending and always iterative, allowing accessible engagement for those who most often find themselves on the outside of formal modes of organizing and development.

Driven by the constant questioning of it, SEA purposefully retains a subversive nature, consistently resisting or dismantling an idea that it can become a closed and defined practice. This nature allows for sustained, accessible and expansive reach to include "unpopular" or unfamiliar voices to continually co-create subjective/subjugated genealogies, which Foucault (1980) recognized and asserted as critical to tactically moving forward through struggle. SEA has been evolving as a liberatory and anti-colonial practice over the years since its raw beginnings in the sixties, experimenting with collective mobilization and participation in creativity as emancipatory. Castellano contends that this has meant not just illuminating the injustices of the colonizer but further integrating and recognizing cultural agency to overcome the individualism and class narrowness of colonial culture. Social change materializes in variable ways, with specificity to location — geographic, social and cultural — in what Castellano calls "homegrown theory and processes of experimentation" (Castellano, 2021, p. 14). Any analysis of SEA then must be careful to consider heterogeneity as a practice impacted by many variables, including place, people and politics. This is partly why it is both challenging and opportune to theorize about SEA as it could/should/would be diversely expressed.

Indeed, hooks (1989) emphasizes the margins as critical sites of resistance that nourish perspectives to imagine alternative worlds. Understanding the margins beyond the common views of deprivation or dependency, to recognize them as a "location of radical openness and possibility" (p. 23), drives intentionality in making **arts-based** engagement accessible. Causevic et al. (2020, p. 5) state that the "histories and knowledges of marginalized communities are the histories and knowledges of the majority of the world" and describe the power of writing from a site of struggle rather than about sites of struggle. hooks (1989) confirms the arts as creative spaces that affirm and sustain subjectivities, where people can articulate pains and struggles but also pleasures, desires and radical imaginings.

Creative, political and intellectual interventions from the margins are increasingly needed in times of growing disparities, tensions and even warfare. What is often under siege is culture as a human right through which to determine one's identity and purpose, to participate in social processes and to find well-being and opportunities to thrive socially, economically and politically. Particularly for those cut off from most political processes, SEA processes offer accessible, healing and creatively discursive ways to reclaim and give voice to identity and culture, and to participate in local development toward social movement changes.

Paulo Helguera (2011) asserts that SEA is located at the intersections of conventional art forms and related disciplines of sociology, anthropology and politics. He encourages it to move beyond creating art for symbolic or representational purposes, toward a collective engagement practice that increases communication and understanding between participants, and to elicit collective problem-solving and action. It is the action of creating artistic work together, incorporating **dialogical** processes in combination with relational aesthetics, that takes SEA beyond an artistic discipline into an active political movement-building platform of knowledge generation and exchange.

Many social movements have arisen over the last many years which share a sharpening focus of fighting against the forces of neoliberal, global capitalism and imperialism rooted in and premised on white supremacy, violence, racism, sexism and classism. These forces dominate economic, political and social spheres and require innovation and creativity in social movements to resist. MacCallum et al. (2009) refer to social innovation as a social relation, as empowerment and as collective agency. Tremblay and Pilati (2013) assert that social innovation only works when social problems are addressed with the people most affected at the centre or in the lead of solutions. Programs that integrate a focus on social innovation can be effective, but often it is organizing outside of institutions or services that is more enduring and compelling for communities, particularly those on the margins with understandable suspicion of institutional structures. As argued in Chapter 2, there is an important need for bringing the "social" back to discussions of "innovation," which involves community-generated solutions and responses.

The engagement of people working together in creative ways beyond governments and authorities is needed for sustained participation in the conjoined struggle against the forces of empire and imperialism. Rojas and Naber (2022) posit that this pointed focus requires contemporary **contentious politics** rooted in a defining praxis of collective coalition building. This praxis is best based on multi-issue, decolonial, anti-imperialist and anti-racist feminist-of-colour organizing that has led change for generations. Self-determined, community-led, creative-strategy building can be networked and connected to not just one movement but rather to many movements that seek to accomplish the unfinished, or rather, ongoing, work of emancipation in which we are all implicated and our presence all required. This lens allows us to contemplate SEA as activities or tactics that are effective and catalytic across many diverse movement repertoires, and that, in aggregate, over time, effectively position SEA as a practice movement in itself.

Bayat (2000) describes practice movements unassumingly as quiet encroachments on normative society, with actions typically appearing in stark contrast to entrenched or unquestioned norms. Practice movements are collective in that individuals are always impacting one another as they share information, skills, knowledge and experience, while inspiring and referring to each other to generate collective identity. Eckert (2015) claims that practice movements are specifically conducive spaces for communities that are largely ignored by dominant society to build capacity, voice and agency to change their situations by taking matters into their own hands. Often seemingly unorganized and unrepresented as collective action, they mostly move for the co-creation of livable lives, "defined by forms of practice that are oriented toward goals that reside above all in some improvement of the everyday possibilities of living" (Eckert, 2015, p. 568). They centre daily actions and relationships that enact movement goals over long periods of activation, often without much fanfare. These movements strive to improve access to material goods, representation, or participation in typically exclusionary systems or institutions. They are fundamentally social, with members articulating visions of possibilities and collaborating in ways to realize those visions. Those involved become empowered as rights-bearing and agential with full capacity to author positive change collectively.

Practice movements based in SEA and led by those on the margins can then enact everyday resistances in relationship building and becoming. As such, SEA builds capacity for creativity, collaboration, empathy, collective care and intimacy that over time generates collective consciousness and new relational norms in social organization. Castellano (2021, p. 9) affirms that SEA practices are "exercises in radical imagination attempting to invent different categories of the human and of human acting and interrelating." SEA becomes a participatory method, hence practice, for "movement actors" to identify with their potential roles in knowledge production and leadership against systems that enact and sustain structural inequalities. Creating a social space/incubator in which those participating are constantly sense-making, theorizing and organizing collective frames to guide their

Pro-Tests and *Making with Place* 41

actions and behaviour, SEA enables generative space for Gramsci's (1971) theory of organic intellectuals to innovate social action and fulfil the tasks of sustained movement action. Wellington Sousa (2022) states that for Gramsci, transformation is based on praxis in which action and thought are connected to create practices that guide social relations. His work supports ideas of spontaneous philosophy and practice for change to be found in the everyday life of ordinary people — in their creativity and common sense that, in coming together, builds critical consciousness, explores cooperative ways of doing life and creates deliberate democracy. This combination of factors, Gramsci contends, is a base for practicing radical concepts for a new society.

Considering SEA as a practice movement legitimizes its role and significance within movement study: it's seen as a mode of civic participation through which marginalized communities assert themselves, thrive and lead. Dean Spade, in their foreword for *Abolition Feminisms* (Bierria et al., 2022), affirms transformative work as happening outside of systems and led most often by people who have been deemed by dominant society to be "disposable." Among calls for systemic change, the most profound, perhaps, is the persistent conviction that answers to injustice rest not with power and authorities, but with people themselves, acting together to recognize truths, restore justice and radically co-create livable and thriving futures beyond inequitable, capitalistic systems. SEA can be seen as a social movement learning and experimentation space that can facilitate the development of organic intellectuals among marginalized communities to move beyond a dominantly perceived state of constant deprivation building their problem-solving agentiality. In this self-organizing and reorganizing active space, they can creatively and dialogically explore their shared experiences and understandings of both real and perceived limits and possibilities. Through this, they create bonds and social cohesion, a unity that is not to be confused with homogenizing sameness, but that differentially unites them in discerning their common goals and shared visions. With time, those involved can self/co-determine their participation in society; in part, they do this through their refusal to participate in the status quo that excludes them. From here, they reorganize or prefigure worlds that defy their social exclusion by virtue of their constant gathering — defining and redefining ways that they want to be together. Relational interactivity in SEA supports iterative meaning-making, participation and decision-making in culture, collective reimaginings and practice space to carve out new pathways. SEA is making and remaking by actively engaging people to chart decolonial paths referred to by Mignolo and Walsh

(2018, p. 25) in "a posture of both protest and proposition" necessary for social change.

We take up these ideas of SEA as a practice movement by evolving a model in phases unfolding along a progressive continuum: "Internal Landscapes," to understand ourselves as meaning-making agents of change and knowledge producers; "Collaborative Activation and Production," as material expressions of collective care in art that moves out from self to community; "Reflection and Theorizing," as collaborative meaning-making that leads to relational becoming and collective identity; and finally, "Collective Action," which builds and sustains radical belonging to spur on actions of change.

INTERNAL LANDSCAPES IN CREATIVE MEANING-MAKING — WHERE THE PRACTICE MOVEMENT BEGINS

We, the artists of *Making with Place* (MWP), came together as researchers to contemplate place during the onset of the COVID-19 pandemic (Lombardo et al., 2023). Social engagement was particularly challenging during isolating lockdowns, quite literally scattering us and keeping us from physically connecting. Our commitment to being present was often interrupted by health constraints, both physiological and psychological, but we pressed on using an online sharing space as a touchstone for sustaining individual creative practice. This space of knowledge-making was consensually agreed upon as a place to share emotions, memories and ideas using various sensory, body and affective means.

Our artworks became talking pieces that facilitated rich dialogue about how place shows up in our internal landscapes and expresses limitations experienced explicitly during the lockdowns and implicitly in colonial violence or in navigating racial oppression and poverty. In her visual art piece *Intrusive Thoughts,* Jess De Vitt creates images of dandelions growing

Figure 1: From left to right: *Intrusive Thoughts* by Jess De Vitt; a drone capture photograph of dancer Nigel Edwards; a photographic diptych by Jahmal Nugent. From *MWP* Research Projects, 2020. Photography by Jahmal Nugent.

through and out of a brain as a way of communicating anxiety and its pervasive disruptions on senses of calm and optimism. Confined to his apartment building, dancer Nigel Edwards one day found his way to the rooftop and began solo movement amidst construction wires and materials. Watching his dance video illuminated for the group how he was making sense of isolation and confinement and allowed us to feel it too. Contemplating these material realities of constraint expressed through art, as meaning-making in this discursive sharing format, ignited our desires and served to deepen our commitments to transcend them. As the weeks progressed through COVID-19 lockdowns, the group's unstoppable creativity became rich food for our souls.

The *MWP* research project created a collective learning space, through which we encouraged and challenged one another to collectively and creatively respond to each other's personal experiences during this time of significant public and social upheaval. Eventually, we activated new spatiality in public space with our art, finding it essential to share our ideas with others.

COLLABORATIVE ACTIVATIONS: *MWP* AND PRODUCTION AS COLLECTIVE CARE

Despite pandemic lockdowns, resulted in sculptural experiments that expressed commitments and intentions for community and culture, beyond virtually mediated sharing space. We worked together to install guerrilla-style subversions of physical and social spaces across the downtown Toronto area. These could be considered small, direct actions, part of social movement repertoire, offering material artworks that engaged the broader community. These works could also be viewed as contentious politics themselves in that during times when public health mandates and repeated lockdowns worked to keep people from gathering, the works disrupted the isolation with expressed invitations to engage, to take part and to receive.

As pictured in Figure 2, Jess De Vitt and Suzie Mensah overlaid text onto an existing mural for *An Invitation,* creating a visual manifesto and call to action to dismantle anti-Black racism. *Medicine Mobiles* and *Dreamcatcher Mobiles,* created by Olympia Trypis, were comprised of small vials containing bits of plants and other natural materials, and dreamcatchers of varying sizes, all hung in artful mobiles and given as gifts to communities of camp dwellers that emerged across the city during the pandemic. Each piece created a unique potential for interaction and relationship. The art pieces evolved through conversations to become outward place-making engagements that needed interaction with others to fulfil their intent. Production

Figure 2: Pictured from left to right: *An Invitation* by Jess De Vitt and Suzie Mensah; *Medicine Mobiles* and *Dreamcatcher Mobiles* by Olympia Trypis. From *MWP* Research Projects, 2020. Photography by Phyllis Novak.

created a kind of interface through which what we practised could move out into the world for further engagement. For example, artist-researcher Jess De Vitt followed her curiosity about dandelions, first appearing in *Intrusive Thoughts* (illustrated in Figure 1), from their colonial dismissal as an invasive weed through to Indigenous uses of the plant as medicine and food. This collaboration with dandelions led to a deeper inquiry into mutual aid, collective care and food justice initiatives with BIPOC leadership. Jess went on to co-create two zines of collective care practices and recipe exchanges with collaborators contributing from as far away as Mexico.

Artist-researchers moved from a place of internal meaning and solo practice to sharing work with others for collective interpretation, production and activation, thereby evolving spheres of relationality and collective care (Lombardo, 2023). Alacovska (2020, p. 727) posits SEA as an ontological phenomenon of caring practice — "a relational practice of sustaining and repairing the world" that asserts creative work as a "labour of compassion" (p. 728). This can be expressed in both the processes involved in SEA, as well as in its material expressions or final productions. SEA, like relational aesthetics, produces a social experience that people can relate to. In this concept, SEA works only become "finished" when animated or engaged with by others, not as spectators to the work, but as both recipients and activators of its fulfilment.

MWP expanded from that first year as a research project with placemaking experiments into the basis for a year-long socially engaged design process to create a series of public art activations. Because lockdowns were still active, making it difficult for young artists to come to social activities or attend programs, SKETCH co-designed in small, curatorial teams that invited young people into design residencies. These residencies at first

Figure 3: *Lokey Care Booth* by artist Logan Marrast. Curated by Jah Grey, this was part of a socially engaged public art installation, *My Public Living Room*, led by Julian Diego from *MWP* Research Projects, 2022. Photography by Jahmal Nugent.

acted very similarly to the research project in that prompts were given and artists created work on their own and shared that work in dialogues activated mostly on Zoom. The curatorial teams listened deeply in those sessions and, from that, they imagined artful activations that could reach out to broader audiences. One such project was *My Public Living Room*, created by a curatorial group who named themselves "The Good Guise."

This group of racialized men and gender-nonconforming folks explored healthy relationships and confronted toxic masculinity. They had vulnerable conversations around what kind of future ancestors they wanted to be. Deep dialogue rooted in community and circle practice led to poetry, rap, music and beatboxing. Within months, the group determined principles for pods of radical care, inspired by HIV/AIDS activists of the 1980s. They chose to make their deliberations public at a small parkette that had been the location of fatal violence to their friends and families involving the police. They desired to bring repair and healing to that site which represented deep grief for the community. They centred their engagement around a decommissioned phone booth encircled by four small wooden benches upon which words were inscribed that declared their mutually agreed-upon principles of transformative community: Care; Accountability; Creativity; and Sustainability.

The phone booth became a micro-gallery with room for one visitor at a time. Inside were photographs of male community members and neighbours, family and friends who offered mentorship, nurturing and a sense of wholeness. In the middle of that park, with the material dark memory of lost loved ones, violence in relationships, systemic racism and uncertainty about identities, the micro-gallery offered brief respite and connection. For "The Good Guise" and for their community, it offered a centring presence affirming personal value and that which makes them whole. The phone booth's light quite literally shone in the darkness, communicating warmth to anyone driving by. From this active installation, hundreds engaged in further conversations through which emerged *The Guise Guide: A Radical Care Zine for Racialized Men*. This guide has since been used in workshops in schools and community centres. Subsequently, a film was made about this journey which travelled to film festivals and received the "Audience Choice Award" at Toronto's "Reel Asian Film Festival" in 2023. The conversation continues — and a movement continues to percolate — that prioritizes transformative justice and collective care at its core to support and encourage racialized men to be leaders in their communities.

Figure 4: A photograph of *Hear Us!* From *Reconstructions of Home*, a public art installation at The Bentway, from *MWP Public Art Projects*, 2021. Photography by Jahmal Nugent.

RELATIONAL BECOMING AND COLLECTIVE IDENTITY —
SPACE FOR THEORIZING TOGETHER

Making with Place invited us into these affective and aesthetic dimensions of knowledge production through multi-layered, embodied analysis (Capous-Desyllas & Bromfield, 2018). Co-production is expressed as an emergent practice of reflective meaning-making that builds on personal relationships of collective care toward collective identity (Groot et al., 2019). In their commitment to these processes, the artists honoured principles of relational ethics and provided a strong foundation for dialogic learning across difference, making space for uncommon voices to be part of the theoretical process leading to collective action (Nicholas et al., 2019; Phillips et al., 2021).

Out of those early production experiments arose themes of houseless communities and displacement. The production site of The Bentway, an urban park in downtown Toronto, had been home to so many whose transience saw them creating temporary shelter under bridges and the expressway on and off ramps. The speed of the cars and trucks above was often said to have created a soothing audio track akin to ocean tides for those sleeping just below. *Reconstructions of Home* sprung from those reflective conversations to further engage those with lived experience as artist-researchers. Panels of collaged imagery in spray paint expressed the volatile feelings that arose recounting multiple experiences of displacement and erasure. Images of ears and mouths opening wide expressed the group's voicelessness, captured in the first piece that emerged called *Hear Us!* (see Figure 4). It features panels surrounded by a painted phone booth with — markedly — no actual phone within it. A phone number and QR code are displayed, leading those who take the time to make the call (assuming access to cell phones) to an audio track of conversations the creative team hosted with houseless folks. While the graffiti-style panels screamed for attention and hearing, the intimacy of the stories reachable only by phone invited those engaged to listen deeply and hold the expressed stories with respect. To launch this "exhibition," a commemorative procession engaged audiences to walk the length under the bridge in solemn remembrance while following a New Orleans blues band. Images of those who had lost their lives to the opioid epidemic and to homelessness flashed in ghostly fashion on screens to the sidelines of the procession.

This immersive enactment of witness eventually led to the curatorial team (comprised of artists with lived experience of homelessness) designing a walking tour under the bridge that invited others in scavenger-hunt format to find posters with embedded augmented reality. The walk and the digital media took participants deep into curated song, story, art and calls to action about homelessness in the city. At their heart, these expressions voiced a simple message of recognizing the value, experiences and contributions to culture of those living houseless. Along the walk was a shipping container, flanked by storage lockers containing miniature dioramas, taking participants yet deeper into conversations of memories. Here, films were screened, panel discussions were hosted and many engaged in making hundreds of small glass vials containing gifts of nature to be given away — a harkening back to the research project that inspired this entire journey.

Over the two years of this iterative project, the stories compiled recommendations for a city-wide coalition that worked together on the expressway corridor plan. This project exemplifies how the art produced was part of a complex conversation that kept unfolding and, with every interaction, evolving into calls to action: first, to look past (or into) the loud and brash voice of homelessness; second, to hear and listen deeply; and third, to walk "in [their] shoes" with commemorative spirit. This experience invited greater awareness and partnership with houseless community members and exemplified the power of people to build up a collective identity and empower it to participate in collective action. (See Chapter 2 for a critical discussion of the need to redefine the "problem" of homelessness from the perspective of those experiencing it.)

Figure 5: Pictured from left to right: *Safe Landing* by Lisa Petrunia; *Being Seen* by Emmet Reed; *Lockers Are Home* by Sue Cohen, all a part of an audio-visual tour called *a wandering* that made up *Reconstructions of Home.* From *MWP* Public Art Projects, 2022. Photography by Phyllis Novak.

COLLECTIVE ACTION TOWARD RADICAL BELONGING — IS THIS NOT THE ULTIMATE AIM OF ALL SOCIAL MOVEMENTS?

Socially engaged art prioritizes transformative care for communities engaging in participatory processes that expand their circles of care and kinship and prioritize reciprocity and interdependence. Indeed, the most long-lasting changes in SEA happen through transformations in care practices that are decolonial, that orient us toward one another and beyond self, strengthening mutuality and solidarity over the long term. Mignolo and Walsh (2018) confirm the importance of attention to those on the margins to "activate new constructions, productions, creation, practices and action-reflection that generates alternatives toward a decolonial otherwise" (p. 29). They contend the necessity of decolonial struggle and historical continuity, affirming that liberation must come "from the ground up, that is from the peoples who for centuries have lived the colonial difference" (p. 24).

Louie et al. (2022) theorize radical belonging in anti-racist learning communities as encompassing social and democratic impacts that come from getting at the root of something and changing its fundamental nature. Radical belonging, integrated into SEA, emphasizes lived experiences as the creative fuel and frame of reference in the inclusive co-construction of visions and actions of what could be.

Queering Place emerged as a *MWP* public art project from the simple prompt, "What does it mean to queer place?" Queer and trans-identifying artists created installation art with medicinal plants in old rubber tires and metal planters. This work started in one liminal space in downtown

Figure 6: Pictured in the centre of Force Field, located in Garrison Common, *Queering Place's Medicine Wheel Garden* was an installation by Logan MacDonald for the "Contact Photography Festival" and and part of *MWP* Public Art Projects (2021). Photograph by Jahmal Nugent.

Figure 7: *Queering Place's Medicine Wheel Garden* on the move, led by Naty Tremblay, part of *MWP* Public Art Projects, 2022. Photography by Jahmal Nugent and Phyllis Novak.

Toronto and then grew to create five subsequent installations to carry on the work in partnering sites through the four directions of the Anishinaabe Medicine Wheel. The evolution of the lively artworks worked to create settings within which this prompt could support conversations across identities in various spaces.

The original *Medicine Wheel Garden* beds became the central meeting place for the project over two years; the project itself migrated with the conversation to take up semi-permanent space near Fort York, a historic military base in Toronto. As the project migrated, the artworks offered more medicinal plants to more queer communities who gathered around it.

An interesting materiality of the project was the reuse of old rubber tires destined for landfill. The artists repurposed them as medicine planters, painting them with brash colours and creating audio recordings that would tell stories of the plants within. The planters became curious assemblages that moved from installation in Garrison Common to occupying parking lots, edges of rivers, ravines and university campuses. They serve as iconic centrepieces to gatherings and dialogues that have been carrying on since the project began. The works and the processes involved have become symbolic of queer place-making and place-knowing that stand out in

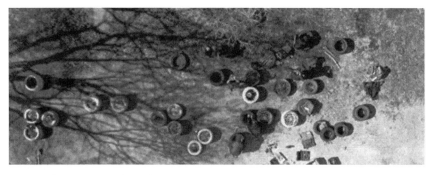

Figure 8: *Queering Place's* Tire Clusters, part of *MWP* Public Art Projects, 2021. Photography by Jahmal Nugent.

Figure 9: *Queering Place* activities, from *MWP* Public Art Projects, 2021 and 2022. From top left to right: tire cluster by Maddie Lycheck; the group in conversation at the west site at Etienne Brule Park; tire cluster by Zephyr Mckenna. On the bottom, from left to right: tire cluster by The Noisewitch; canoeing the plants up Humber River; tire planter by Bert Whitecrow. Photography by Jahmal Nugent and Phyllis Novak.

places where one might least expect them. The medicines that have been on the move have offered various iterations of the initial idea of exploring the medicines that exist in queer identities for world-building. The medicines further ensure that queer communities have what they need to participate in community building in the collective space that has typically othered them or excluded them entirely. It has also been for our own collective liberation.

CONCLUSION

Mignolo and Walsh (2018) emphasize new relational paradigms as necessary in resurgence and insurgence to interrupt colonial ideas and assumptions, and to open up spheres of decolonial thinking and doing. Castellano conceives of socially engaged art as a set of located transgressive actions that seek to challenge visible and not-so-visible forms of coloniality. He affirms SEA as facilitating powerful space and processes through which "common ground and collective power and voice can be negotiated and articulated" (Castellano, 2021, p. 4). When engaging the power of imagination and enacting agential leadership of those who are on the margins, SEA becomes subversive and collaborative, artistic creativity that is politically urgent and carries with it transformative potential for "retooling our conceptual repertoire for epistemic and embodied decolonization" (2021, p. 5).

This connection with decolonial thought and praxis situates SEA as a method to build anti-elitist understandings and to create and facilitate decolonial ethos and aesthetics (breaking individualism and foregrounding the inter-relationality of all beings) to shape ideas of collective agency and social transformation. These ultimately contest what Mignolo and Walsh (2018) refer to as the "totalizing claims and political-epistemic violence of modernity/coloniality" (Mignolo & Walsh, 2018, p. 1) and transcend Western ideas that have organized and sought to control thought and action. This transcendence allows multiple and localized voices to co-create their own "houses of thought" (p. 7). Herein lies the power to move society toward liberation and inclusion, confronting dominant ideologies and dismantling their homogeneity in favour of diverse and subjective knowledges. In particular, for those who have been oppressed, this transcendence provides the opportunity to lead the way.

More studies are needed around SEA as a practice movement and how its practices work to move change. Certainly, the collective consciousness and social organization experienced in SEA nurtures the capacity for creativity, empathy, care and intimacy. Through this chapter, we have expressed the various phases along a continuum of iterative practice that outlines what happens in SEA that can move change. Figure 10 seeks to synthesize and offer key points of our discussion and findings as an iterative and cyclical process.

We argue that a practice movement in SEA starts with creative meaning-making of one's own internal landscape. It is here in explorations through all kinds of art modalities that individuals express stories, discover their creative agency and explore their potential roles in the processes for change. Here, they can find a voice to express grievances or deprivations that lead to expressed needs for change.

Along a continuum from individual to community is a movement from solo practice or art making into collaborative art production to enact collective care. Groups form around common experiences and engage one another in reflexive dialogues, building critical consciousness and unifying their desires to act against injustice and oppressive power. As these groups create together over time, as they enact their sense of collective care through artful iterations and dialogic engagement, they build strength and collaboration around their shared grievances and values. Strong reciprocal relationships and collective imaginations begin to take shape in which collaborators can see, taste and feel the possibilities of their actions together to make change. Their power as a collective supersedes their individual identities. Through this continuum, art interventions and co-created works build on each other and the processes of making them are just as critical as the products created.

The final phase represents collective action and the radical belonging that is experienced as a result. At this point along the practice continuum, sustained actions bring about innovations that express solidarity. Loosely inferred with the twirl at the end of the continuum (see the diagram) is the notion that this practice keeps growing and engaging new members along the way who experience its iterative phases. It is never finished, and we see material and resource changes that improve the everyday realities of those involved. The practice that evolves is one of producing contexts and experiences of possibility and collective presence, that are reflected on and expanded. Change is not necessarily dramatic in any one instance, not one single "innovation," but aggregate change is, in fact, revolutionary, as those often deemed as outside of change-making can become the authors of their own vital and desirable futures while also pointing the way for others to follow.

Novak and Lombardo's model, pictured in Figure 10, builds on earlier iterations used to express the experiences of the *Making with Place* research project (Lombardo, 2023; Lombardo et al., 2023). During the pandemic,

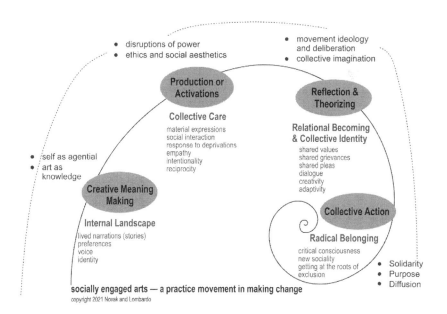

Figure 10: "Socially engaged arts: A practice movement in making change," by Phyllis Novak and Charlotte Lombardo.

MWP engaged young artists on the margins in creative processes that moved beyond solo practice to producing powerful, public art pieces involving over sixty artists and over twenty community members. It was more than artful place-making or participatory art process. Over its three-year span, it opened many opportunities for all involved to play different roles and recognize the connections among their creativity, the surfacing of critical knowledges, and the potentials of art in the public realm — in process and product — for prefiguration through to the creation of counter-narratives. The works supported subsequent individual and group opportunities that included artists teaching and presenting in postsecondary institutions about their experiences and their uses of art in social change. This has opened connections of knowledge exchange between community and academia among other civic partnerships that vitally seek to centre knowledge and leadership from the margins in and for social change.

The need to invigorate and tap into the imagination is key to social movements and social innovation. It enables movement actors to hold on to a collective "us" and a collective "we" that remembers experiences of injustice while reconstructing images and ideas of desirable futures. Hawlina et al., (2020) write that collective imagination in social movements travels across temporalities between the past, the current state and visions of the future. Expanding and nurturing that imagination, that sense of "we" — and, moreover, how one fits into that "we" — are central to movements. Collective identity and collective imagination lead to social cohesion embedded in culture, and this social cohesion is one of the desired impacts of social innovation. SEA facilitates this social cohesion for communities that are most cut off from local development by making space within which their rights to culture, both participation and leadership in it, are recognized as essential to development, even if or perhaps even more so because it is often happening outside of mainstream systems and institutions. The social aesthetics that arise from intentional dialogical and creative engagement among those navigating the margins involve critical consciousness to address social issues and amplify or create new practices generated within these communities. (See Chapter 2 for further discussion of social aesthetics.) Practices that demonstrate belonging in the radical sense — relational connections to overall collective purposes that get at the root of social inequalities and exclusions. These visions not only improve the quality of life for those most marginalized, they also critically attend to inequitable structures and help the community carry on despite and beyond them.

The rigour needed to combat and overcome ongoing systems of "empire" takes repeated effort, practice, storytelling and undoing of many kinds. These actions, collectively combined and enacted over and over, engender an ethos of politicized respect, care and appreciation for processes. This ethos, in turn, enables truths to be told, survivance and fortitude to be recognized and collective imagination to be ignited. There is, after all, much experience to be expressed, recognized and repaired. There are also many re-makings needed that involve paradigm-shifting relationality, where no one is left behind and where people are sought out and supported for their creativity despite pervasive oppressive systems and politics or circumstances of exclusion.

Socially engaged arts is participatory action, not "service," and it is not merely an innovation tactic, although it can satisfy those. It is innovation-in-constant-making that makes way for sociality and co-creation for deliberation and to serve activist aims, which insists on constant critical examinations of hegemonic power. It emphasizes mutuality and solidarity and invites multiple, accessible modes for insurgent political, epistemic and praxis-based diffusions that affect change in deep and lasting ways. As such, we would argue for its further study and investment among marginalized communities so that they will be resourced to tap into their radical leadership to prefigure ways and means toward their collective liberation.

Reflection Questions

1. What does "the margins" mean to you and why is this concept important for movement-making?
2. How do socially engaged arts (SEA) inform and expand ideas of social innovation?
3. In what ways can SEA projects like *Making with Place* help us engage with and enact practice movements as social innovation for social change?

ACKNOWLEDGEMENTS

We write this chapter with deep gratitude to the artist-researchers: Jess De Vitt, Ayrah Taerb, Olympia Trypis, Jahmal Nugent, Ammarah Syed, Bert Whitecrow, Pree Rehal and Nigel Edwards, for their community-activist scholarship that they exercise through new art creations that work toward social change. They are indeed leaders of many movements in their communities. From 2021 to 2022, *Making with Place* public art projects grew to engage over forty artists, collectives and partners (see sketch.ca/publicart/).

56 INTERRUPTING INNOVATION

Gratitude is also extended to SKETCH Working Arts for creating a social innovation incubation space where many of us have tinkered away at developing this critical practice — completely transferable to multiple contexts and ever-ready to be shared. For more information, please see SKETCH's website at sketch.ca, and the MWP website at makingwithplace.ca.

REFERENCES

Alacovska, A. (2020). From passion to compassion: A caring inquiry into creative work as socially engaged art. *Sociology, 54*(4), 727–744.

Bayat, A. (2000). From 'dangerous classes' to 'quiet rebels': Politics of the urban subaltern in the Global South. *International Sociology, 15*(3), (2000), 533–557.

Bishop, C. (2012). *Artificial hells: Participatory art and the politics of spectatorship.* Verso.

Bierria, A., Caruthers, J., & Lober, B. (Eds.) (2022). *Abolition feminisms: Vol. 1. Organizing, survival and transformative practice.* Haymarket Books.

Castellano, C.G. (2021). *Art activism for an anticolonial future.* State University of New York Press.

Causevic, A., Philip, K., Zwick-Maitreya, M., Hooper Lewis, P., Bouterse, S., & Sengupta, A. (2020). Centering knowledge from the margins: our embodied practices of epistemic resistance and revolution. *International Feminist Journal of Politics, 22*(1), 6-25.

Foucault, M. (1980). Two lectures. In G. Colin (Ed.), *Power/knowledge: Interviews and other writings 1972-1977* (pp. 78-108). Random House.

Goeman, M. (2013). *Mark my words: Native women mapping our nations.* University of Minnesota Press.

Gramsci, A., Hoare, Q., & Nowell-Smith, G. (1971). *Selections from the prison notebooks of Antonio Gramsci (1st ed.).* Lawrence & Wishart.

Hawlina, H., Clifford Pedersen, O., & Zittoun, T. (2020). Imagination and social movements. *Current Opinion in Psychology, 35,* 31–35.

Helguera, P. (2011). *Education for socially engaged art.* Jorge Pinto Books.

hooks, bell. (1989). Choosing the margin as a space of radical openness. *Framework: The Journal of Cinema and Media, 36,* 15–23.

hooks, bell. (1984). *Feminist theory: From margin to centre.* South End Press.

Kester, G.H. (2011). *The one and the many: Contemporary collaborative art in a global context.* Duke University Press.

Lombardo, C. (2023). *Making with place: Youth artist researchers as creative agents of change.* [Doctoral dissertation]. York University. hdl.handle.net/10315/41797.

Lombardo, C., Novak, P., Flicker, S., & *Making with Place* Artists. (2023). Making with Place: Youth public art experiments. *Art/Research International: A Transdisciplinary/ Journal, 8*(1), 142–172.

Louie, N., Berland, L., Roeker, L., Nichols, K., Pacheco, M., & Grant, C. (2022). Toward radical belonging: Envisioning antiracist learning communities. *Race, Ethnicity and Education* (forthcoming), 1–21.

Maccallum, D., Moulaert, F., Hillier, J., & Vicarihaddock, S. (2009). *Social innovation and territorial development.* Ashgate.

Mignolo, W.D., & Walsh, C.E. (2018). *On decoloniality.* Duke University Press.

Rojas, C., & Naber, N. (2022). Genocide and "US" domination (is not equal to) liberation. Only we can liberate ourselves. In A. Bierria, J. Caruthers, & B. Lober (Eds.), *Abolition feminisms vol. 1: Organizing, survival, and transformative practice* (pp. 6-8). Haymarket Books.

Spade, D. (2022). Foreword. In A. Bierria, J. Caruthers, & B. Lober (Eds.), *Abolition feminisms vol. 1: Organizing, survival, and transformative practice* (pp. 8-9). Haymarket Books.

Tremblay, D-G., & Pilati, T. (2013). Social innovation through arts and creativity. In F. Moulaert, D. MacCallum, A. Mehmood, & A. Abdel Hamdouch (Eds.), *International handbook on social innovation. social innovation, collective action and transdisciplinary research* (pp. 67–79). Edward Elgar Publishing.

Wellington Sousa, J. (2022). Liberating community-based research: Rescuing Gramsci's legacy of organic intellectuals. *Engaged Scholar Journal: Community-Engaged Research, Teaching, and Learning, 8*(3), 1–17.

Considering Networked Responses as Social Innovation

Case Examples of Incels, Amazon's Ring and Community Care

Lauren Morris, Al Cunningham Rogers and Quinn MacNeil

> **Learning Objectives**
> 1. Be able to define "transformative social innovation" and provide examples.
> 2. Learn how to apply theories of social innovation to analyze a case example.
> 3. Identify some of the unintended consequences of social innovation and processes of empowerment.

THIS CHAPTER EXPLORES THREE CASE EXAMPLES of transformative social innovation that alter dominant institutions by changing social relations within a community of actors (Avelino et al., 2019). Taken together, these case studies suggest that the social practices of specific actors — such as the online forums created by **incel** communities; the collective vigilance and sharing of smart doorbell surveillance footage; and the collective care practices of **Mad/Disabled** communities — can be understood as socially innovative in the ways that they change social relations and shift institutional dynamics. The case studies also point to the way that, as Avelino et al. (2019) note, social innovation is not inherently beneficial for all and can lead to both empowering and disempowering effects, depending on the ways social innovation is taken up by disparate actors and communities. In offering these three examples of social innovation, we invite the reader to reflect critically on the multiple, and at times contradictory, outcomes of social innovation.

Taking up this collection's inquiry into the connection between social innovation and social justice, which understands social innovation to be collective action, this chapter argues for the need for critical perspectives on social innovation as collective action because these movements can be co-opted by neoliberal governments, corporations and others for personal gain and profit. As forms of collective action and social activism, socially innovative practices can address community needs through a lens of autonomy and empowerment, but they can also be used to police the borders of community and reinforce existing power imbalances.

Each of the three examples presented provide a critical examination of the concepts of empowerment and increased autonomy. In the preceding chapters, the authors explored examples of community-based initiatives that also address autonomy, empowerment and greater participation. They also highlight some of the potential pitfalls of social innovation when it does not begin with a challenge to the status quo. Continuing in this vein, these case studies take up how social innovation, even when action is meant to be empowering or to increase community autonomy, can have unintended, negative consequences. Taken together, the case studies highlight the complicated impacts of socially innovative practices and how these practices can be taken up by external actors for personal benefit.

The first example offers a discussion of reactionary agitation against the empowerment of women. In online forums, involuntary celibate men — calling themselves "incels" — believe themselves to be victimized by social innovations brought about by what they describe as the "Western feminist social movement." They perceive these innovations to have allowed women to exercise an "unfairly" high degree of sexual autonomy and economic power. They also tend to believe that these innovations in socio-economic relations have been disempowering for a majority of men (but particularly for them) because incels locate themselves at the bottom of a supposed social hierarchy, which they believe privileges women and physically attractive, wealthy, dominant men. Within this nihilistic embrace of powerlessness, some incels articulate their resistance through the language of "laying down to rot": a deliberate refusal to participate in the economy or engage with masculine productivity roles. While "laying down to rot" serves as an example of collective action embodied in a mass refusal to engage, contradicting narratives within the community can also orient misogynistic incels toward re-asserting masculine power through acts of violence. In either case, these strategies for social innovation are rooted in the incels' perceived exclusion from a masculine "right" to hold social and economic power.

In the second example, Amazon's Ring Video Doorbell (Ring) mobilizes a narrative of empowerment for its users to be active participants in their own safety/risk management by emphasizing their agency to check camera feeds and share content with their online community. However, community members are disempowered to build deeper relationships with one another through the one-sided surveillance afforded by the platform. Instead of engaging with community members, Ring encourages users to scrutinize passersby and to create meaning from what enters the frame of the camera, thereby mediating relationships based on visible attributes and contextless behaviour. Additionally, Ring increases population productivity by emphasizing and encouraging the circulation of recorded "disorderly behaviour." The characterization of disorderly behaviour has historically been vulnerable to elite interests in preserving the appearance of a safe space to do business — see the example of responses to homelessness critiqued in Chapter 2. When normative uses of space and indicators of insecurity are established, the "disorderly body" becomes the target of initiatives that either force them to conform to the defined order, or alternatively, require them to adopt a peripheral existence to avoid disciplinary action.

Similarly, the Disability Rights Movement and Mad/Disabled communities' calls for increased autonomy over the administration of their own care have led to the development of the Direct Funding Program in Ontario, which gives qualifying Disabled service users the direct administrative control they asked for. However, alongside their promise of providing the users with increased choice and autonomy, Direct Funding has also offloaded the administrative labour of care onto Disabled people and communities who are now responsibilized for their care (Hande & Kelly, 2015). Alongside community mobilizations to increase service user choice and autonomy over care, Direct Funding also works to uphold neoliberal ideas of individual responsibility and the continued shrinking of the government-administered social welfare state, using a narrative of "care empowerment" that positions self-administration as an opportunity for increased control and decision-making.

In the two examples of "transformative" social innovation, where greater empowerment and autonomy have been sought, and in the example of a reaction to empowering social innovation, one is witness to how community formations dictate the boundaries of community, identifying who is included in shared social spaces. As collective action, transformative social innovation both operationalizes social relationships within communities while reproducing power imbalances. Transformative social innovation as a process that acts on social relations to meet a shared goal or need can have diverse and at times unintended consequences.

THEORETICAL UNDERPINNINGS: A CRITICAL UNDERSTANDING OF SOCIAL INNOVATION

Critical scholars have begun to contest a once-widespread assumption that social innovation is necessarily desirable and always leads to social benefits (Fougere & Merilainen, 2021). Arguing that social innovation can lead to unintended or other detrimental social consequences, Avelino et al. (2019, p. 198) argue that socially innovative practices are simply defined by the ways they "challenge/alter/replace existing social relations and practices." They describe transformative social innovation as practices which challenge/alter/replace dominant institutions while changing the way people do things.

Thus, social innovation is not necessarily empowering, but rather transforms social relations and contests the boundaries of power in some way. For example, social innovation can work to increase productivity, in what Fougere and Merilainen (2021, p. 13) describe as increasing "productive power" by "help[ing] marginalized people become better integrated in a society." Narratives of empowerment and other discourses surrounding social innovation can be hijacked by powerful actors to drive "their own interests of capital accumulation while calling for communities to self-organize" (p. 1).

Social innovation and associated changes in the dynamics of social relations can have both empowering and disempowering effects, have unintended counter-effects or may "not necessarily lead to desirable social goals" (Avelino et al., 2019, p. 199). Chapter 2 takes up some of these unintended consequences of innovation, especially when it eschews the "social." Similarly, the examples presented in this chapter encourage the reader to think critically about the varying effects of socially innovative movements: how discourses of power and empowerment operate within social groups and how these movements might be co-opted by external actors for personal benefit or to uphold the status quo.

NEOLIBERALISM AS A SHAPING FORCE

As both an economic and social force, neoliberalism shapes us as enmeshed bodies and minds — "bodyminds" (Nishida, 2016) — including our beliefs, desires and behaviours, thereby impacting the ways in which we organize and care for one another. The way we imagine who is in our community and who shares our values, needs and goals shapes the way we practice social innovation on a wider scale. While it might not be readily apparent what incel subforums, disability care collectives and corporate surveillance technologies have in common, this chapter will demonstrate how each community takes up or reacts to innovative practices to address structural problems caused by neoliberal conditions. In each example, narratives of autonomy and empowerment are used to operationalize communities toward non-participation as resistance; surveillance as safety; and self-administration as choice in care provision.

What we care about, and what is framed as a social problem that needs to be addressed on a community level, are influenced by neoliberalism and the data economy. Using social innovation as a critical framework to assess this impact, and the ways communities are responding to social forces, helps us identify some of the real-world consequences that larger social structures such as neoliberalism have on the ways people organize and how social narratives are formed. When thinking about what communities care for and what issues or common goals they choose to mobilize around, one should recall that social relations are never neutral and that the ways we care for each other in community are bound up with other systems of power. As we will see, interrogating the structures and relations through which communities actualize a social goal can help identify the ways that power operates in social space.

Neoliberal ideology elevates entrepreneurialism and risk-taking while maintaining self-sufficiency and responsibility as demanded by the devolution of government welfare and support (Marwick, 2013). With the goal of producing good corporate citizens, neoliberalism is reified through "policies and processes whereby a relative handful of private interests are permitted to control as much as possible of social life in order to maximize their personal profit" (McChesney, 1999, p. 40). Neoliberal capitalism is therefore not just an analytical framework for economic organization but is also a normative structure that provides a framework for how society is organized. Under neoliberalism, the market provides the overriding ethical context, outlining an ideal for social organization while endorsing and naturalizing an entrepreneurial individualism that is self-interested (Lynch, 2021). Guided by critical understandings of social innovation and the role of neoliberalism, the three case examples invite the reader to consider the multiple and divergent outcomes of socially innovative practices and how narratives of empowerment can be operationalized to reproduce power imbalances across different contexts.

CASE EXAMPLE I: INCELS

Incels are "terminally online," mostly young, avowedly cis-gender and performatively straight men experiencing difficulties achieving romantic and sexual relationships, often to the point of lacking all such experiences.

They have a sense of aggrieved entitlement (Kimmel, 2013), which seems to arise from a perception that they have been unfairly denied sexual and romantic connections. Many use the online incel community as a place to vent about feelings of loneliness, social alienation and a lack of solid kinship networks. Some adherents to the incelibate ideology, including the self-avowed and those posthumously inducted by the community, have been responsible for acts of **spectacularized violenc**e (Cottee, 2020; Hoffman, Ware, & Shapiro, 2020; Witt, 2020) in Canada and the US (BBC, 2018; CBC/Radio Canada, 2018; Brockbank, 2019; CBC, 2019; Ankel, 2020; BBC, 2020). Incels see lashing out by punishing **normie** women and men with violence as a means of anti-feminist social innovation. On the other end of the spectrum, incels who "lay down to rot" practice an extreme social withdrawal from kin networks, employment and education, leading toward the total siloing of social interrelations onto mediated platforms of incel forums, video games and pornography.

While Mad and Disabled communities marginalized by neoliberal economics have creatively used networked community infrastructure to enable resource sharing, misogynist incels converge online to share their grievances in what Cottee describes as a "wound culture" (2020, p. 14). These incel counter-narratives of masculine grievance are reactionary, emerging in response to economic trends that have seen women gain degrees of social and economic power. Notwithstanding the disparate distribution of any gains made under feminist waves of progress toward different groupings of women, incels perceive it in totality to have come as a loss to the group status of men. In a historically revisionist effort at positioning themselves as disempowered by past waves of economic systems change, incels claim a moral right to argue for reparations. And given a deeply felt sense of nihilistic helplessness, the incel believes himself to be left with two options: lash out or lay down.

The internet enables many possible opportunities for collective action, as the subsequent cases will examine. Its impacts upon the changing shape of social relations have yet to be fully mapped. One potentially negative transformation in social relations is a state of doom-scrolling, which emerges as a potential subject position in the internet era. To doom-scroll is to consume mediated content on a mobile device, even while experiencing what Crary (2013, pp. 87–89) describes as "a flattening of response and the replacement of pleasure with the need for repetition." Using the affectively tinted subject position of doom-scrolling, we can explore one manifestation of an effort at changing the terms of social relations: doom-scrolling as the strategy of incels who "lay down and rot."

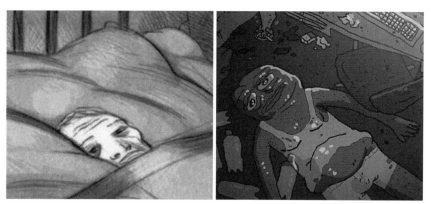

Figure 11: "Lay Down and Rot" Memes, from Incels.wiki.

"Lay Down and Rot" (LDAR), the mantra for a segment of the misogynist incel population, "is a state of being that a person may reach if they conclude there is no point to striving after success and accomplishment" ("Lay Down and Rot," Incels.wiki., n.d.). LDAR is a fatalistic retreat from society. It is distinguishable from a clinical diagnosis of depression in that it is more than a collection of symptoms — it is additionally a choice justified by a political ideology. Characteristics of LDAR include: rotting in bed alone; isolating from friends and family; connecting with others only through the "cocoons of control and personalization" (Crary, 2013, p. 87), granted by the insularity of internet communities; and the detrimental overconsumption of video games and pornography.

There is a thread to be teased out here: though LDAR incels want to "lay/lie in bed" and "rot," this action is not synonymous with sleep, rest or rejuvenation. One shift associated with neoliberal market transformations has been the erosion of sleep time and quality, associated with what Crary (2013, p. 28) identifies as "24/7 time." Where consumption and production interactions are always available, endlessly solicited and never really finished, sleep time is put off, shrunk and sought to be done away with for good. One way that we might feel "24/7 time" is in the act of cross-platform doom-scrolling — the sleepless, joyless, endless consumption of media. To rot is to isolate from social life, but to rest is to become vulnerable in the care of others. Consider how a collective strategy that sought to protect sleep time might also protect and strengthen our interpersonal relationships, improve our physical and mental health and aid in our ability to resist the alienating individualization of neoliberal capitalism.

What kind of social relations are practised (or not) by LDAR incels? What sort of a world is this an argument for? Because it is assuredly a "change in social relations, involving new ways of doing, organising, knowing and framing" (Avelino et al., 2019, p. 197), even if it is a profoundly disempowering one. Attempts at changing the terms of social relations by retreating behind walls of technological mediation and managing relations through "cocoons of control and personalization" (Crary, 2013, p. 87) can also manifest in other communities, like the Japanese phenomenon of hikikomori or the alienating and isolating practices associated with Amazon Ring, described in the subsequent case. These communities also turn to networked, information communication technologies to address an apparent need for a feeling of safety and control. These collective shifts in how these communities conduct their social relations could be explained as a response to the anxious and unstable conditions of economic life under late capitalism, as exacerbated by the atomizing and alienating philosophy of neoliberal individualism — and for incels, worsened by sealing themselves in a pressure cooker of online anonymity, rabid conspiracy, misogyny and racism.

The embodied anxiety commonly experienced by subjects living under late-stage, neoliberal capitalism has been well documented. Mark Fisher (2009, pp. 2–5) describes the sentiment of living in the neoliberal condition as "capitalist realism," a "widespread sense" that "capitalism is the only viable political and economic system":

> [It] has become impossible to imagine a coherent alternative [...]. The feeling that there is nothing new [...]. [It] presents itself as a shield protecting us from the perils posed by belief itself. The attitude of ironic distance proper to postmodern capitalism is supposed to immunise us against the seduction of fanaticism.

An attitude of ironic distance is contained within the capitalist, realist mindset, and it fuels the innovation strategies of misogynist incels. (Post)-ironic, "dark," "edge-lord" humour dominates the corners of the internet where incels lurk; this is the kind of humour that gives us racist Pepe memes, the OK hand symbol as a plausibly deniable neo-nazi dog whistle, **Chad** vs. incel vs. **Stacy** memes and the **alpha-beta-sigma mythology** of masculinity. Extending Fisher's conclusion here, an "attitude of ironic distance" is "supposed to immunise us against the seduction of fanaticism" (p. 5, emphasis added), but it does not. Instead of immunization from fanaticism, ironic distance for incels is a mechanism of radicalization — and a means of re-ordering social relations.

What does "laying down and rotting" sound like if not the response of a disillusioned neoliberal subject, struck low by the realization of their impotence? The internalization of an apparent inability to effect change, at a systemic, communal or individual level? LDAR is a prescriptive strategy, a "cope," that for some misogynist incels works to protect them from the ego-death of social alienation. LDAR incels have given up on attempts at "looksmaxxing," learning "game" to pick up women or seeking status in other ways. LDAR as a narrative is employed to justify opting out of neoliberal economic production: it is, as such, a collective action addressing a problem for these individuals with the goal of changing their immediate and extended social relations to better accommodate their group. It reflects a way for this community to practice self-care and seek out a feeling of safety. Yet, their refusal to participate under the current economic and social conditions is also articulated as a condemnation of the validity of the whole system.

The innovative strategies employed by incels can be starkly disparate. Within parts of the community, incel-motivated killers are celebrated as saints and martyrs for the cause (Witt, 2020). These collective acts of stochastic terror are intended to draw attention to the plight of the incelibate; lashing out is a manifest argument for changes to gendered and sexual social institutions, for the symbolic restoration of "lost" masculine power. Accordingly, lashing out with violence could be interpreted as an argument about care: care for "imperilled" masculinity and the perceived declining status of men. As the third case example in this chapter will address in more detail, care is tied up with **systemic power** and is about determining who and what should be carried forward into the future. As such, the stochastic terrorism associated with misogynist incelibacy is a twisted form of expressing care for a lost version of masculinity and an attempt to police the shifting boundaries of gendered and sexual institutions so as to restore masculine power — in effect, to make women and girls afraid again.

This case example has addressed misogynist incels as a community because the forms of collective action for which the misogynist incel ideology tends to argue can cause harm to the rest of us. While LDAR incels seem to mostly hurt themselves, there are some who respond to what they perceive as socio-economic problems brought about by feminism with violence. These arguments, made violently manifest, have transformed social narratives and institutions in ways we cannot reverse, permeating our imaginaries of the future and reshaping current-day legislation.

To lay down and rot, or to turn to spectacular violence, these are attempts to ameliorate the problems that misogynist incels think they face. Yet apathy is not a particularly creative practice, and the acts of spectacularized mass violence are not likely to reconfigure social relations in a healthy way. But Crary describes sleep as one of the last forms of time that has not and cannot be put to service by capital, and further notes how "the imaginings of a future without capitalism begin as dreams of sleep" (2013, p. 126). To be placed in the position of doom-scroller, however, is to rot from lack of rest and incels locate themselves here as a strategy to cope with the social alienation and anxiety felt by the neoliberal subject. Rather than these strategies, might there instead be a form of transformative collective action that seeks to reconstitute social withdrawal as "resting-with," instead of "rotting-alone," that draws a line between the hours of online/offline, sleep/waking, and defends that barrier as a matter of radical collective care?

In all three case examples, collective action taken by a social group works to meet community needs for safety, care and belonging. However, incels and Ring users share a particular preoccupation with space and its control. In the withdrawal into bedrooms and networked online communities, and in the invisible boundaries constructed by Ring around the home, we see the operations of personal strategies to enact control over social relations, including the deployment of narratives that define and redefine the self and (dangerous) others. In the spectacularized acts of mass violence practised by some misogynist incels, and in the capture and recirculation of "disorderly" bodies imaged by doorbell cameras, we also find attempts toward reshaping the way we use and understand not only space, but other people: we see how we move through public spaces, and observe our expectations about what might happen there; we notice the spaces that we consider to be public, private or dangerous; we learn who we consider belonging in the space and who we view as a threat to it.

CASE EXAMPLE II: AMAZON'S RING

This case example examines community safety efforts practised through the adoption of Amazon's smart doorbell, Ring, as a form of empowering collective action and social innovation. We examine how platform-based community safety efforts, such as those mediated through Ring, have altered the social relationships between community members in order to meet the collective goal of enhancing community safety. While the collective action of incels relies on a reclamation of their power through acts of violence or laying down and rotting, Ring users are sold ideas of empowerment and autonomy through the marketing of real-time responsibility and control as a response to users' perceived danger and insecurity. We explore how

68 INTERRUPTING INNOVATION

adopting Ring's surveillance-based approach to community safety can lead to community fracturing through a responsibilized individuated public, while corporations co-opt collective action for their own gain.

Ring was not always sold as a community safety tool. Initially launched as Doorbot in 2012, Ring echoed the neoliberal promise to help customers save time and enhance productivity through a convenient new product. Described as "caller-ID for the front door" by Ring's founder Jamie Siminoff, the selling point was to streamline answering the door by cutting out distracting interactions and by ensuring the important ones, notably deliveries, were not missed. These interests were reflected in Ring's first slogan: "Never miss a visitor." In 2016, the Alexa Fund, Amazon's venture capital arm that invests in products that can be integrated with Alexa voice activation, made an undisclosed investment in Ring. Leading up to Amazon's 2018 acquisition of Ring, the company's visitor-oriented slogan was replaced with a new one: "Your Ring of security starts at the front door." Later, Ring published a mission statement on its website: "To reduce crime in neighborhoods."

This new language positioned Ring as a corporation working toward a social goal, akin to the mission of a non-profit. Through this community safety narrative, Ring began partnering with grassroots community organizations that saw it as a solution to crime and with over two thousand American police agencies that saw it as a tool to identify crime and quantify police efforts. These partnerships helped legitimize Ring's claim of being a means to safer spaces and in some states have even led to the public subsidization of Ring products. To aid this "mission,'" Ring released a host of other security devices, pushing them in bundles with Amazon's Echo speaker, and expanded its partnerships by making Ring compatible with smart locks already established in the market. This networked interoperability allowed Ring to offer new features, such as allowing Amazon Prime delivery drivers to enter private indoor and outdoor spaces to help avoid package theft, one of Amazon's biggest problems as an online retailer — how convenient for them. With more products came more footage for users to assess and share, thereby affording Ring a surplus of scrapable user data with each post on top of its product and monthly subscription revenue. By increasing the volume of footage that relied on Amazon's AWS server for users to store and review clips, the collective action of users to watch and share "suspicious activity" was co-opted by Ring to suit Amazon's growth model. Instead of highlighting Amazon's economic interests in increasing server storage fees and selling data to third parties when content was circulated, these interests were obfuscated in favour of heightening community fear to encourage and moralize the sharing of content.

With the rise in online retail coupled with the COVID-19 pandemic shopping restrictions, porch pirates quickly became a topic of corporate and political interest. From 2019 to 2023, eight states in the US passed legislation to classify this new criminal category as a felony (Thuy Vo, 2022). While stealing mail delivered by the US Postal Service was already designated as a felony, the new legislation expanded the statute to include private carriers such as Amazon. To support this amendment, porch piracy was framed as organized crime instead of opportunistic theft. This rhetoric helped move porch piracy in public consciousness from petty theft to a crime that was deserving of collective action. Using porch pirates as an ample jumping-off point, Ring began to expand its theoretical applications to crime prevention and safety. By building a company ethos around the concept of community safety instead of the minimizing of a particular crime (package theft), Ring was winning consensus that it could facilitate collective action (via sharing content) and combat feelings of insecurity associated with crime.

Feelings of insecurity are constructed through discourse — through how we talk about crime and those who do crimes — regardless of their material impacts on safety. This discourse plays a significant role in determining who/what/where is perceived as potentially dangerous. Community safety is thus very much about creating a perception of safety by addressing a perception of insecurity — making "community safety" susceptible to being appropriated by corporations who use feelings of insecurity and fear to frame problems and commodify solutions.

Daniel Gilling (2001), a professor of criminal justice, has argued that the vagueness and perceived public value of "community safety" make it susceptible to bolstering initiatives that are void of real impact. Community safety initiatives form a difficult discursive arena because opposing voices can quickly be aligned with being on the side of the alternative — crime and danger. This binary logic lures many people into willfully adopting added responsibility or purchasing products such as Ring to "do their part" to help achieve shared social goals through the perceived collective action of sharing, commenting and "watching the neighbourhood" online. Community safety is thus a powerful, neoliberal, rhetorical tool for decentralizing responsibilities as average citizens are "empowered" to take on the responsibility of crime prevention and its costs through private industry–individual partnerships. Policing can be performed by anyone intending to establish, maintain or enforce a defined order or all norms (implicit or explicit) that are designed to regulate behaviour (Hermer et al., 2005, p. 23). As a policing tool, Ring executes a defined order by increasing the spaces and bodies that can be seen, thereby subjecting those captured by its lenses to normative readings and uses of space.

As Avelino et al. (2019) identified, social innovation may be directed toward an identified problem in the current social system. Gilling (2001) importantly addresses this idea of problems by emphasizing that we must ask which groups have the most social power to establish their insecurity as the collectively agreed upon problem to be addressed. He argues that "the evidence suggests it is the insecurity not of the victims of neoliberalism (the socially dislocated underclass), but of the 'respectable classes,' whose enhanced freedom and affluence has come at the expense of growing insecurity about the dangerous other" (p. 397).

However, it is not only a question of which group has the most social power to establish their insecurity as the one to be addressed, but also whose insecurity can be generated into capital. Those whose insecurity can be profitable will be those "whose behaviour is increasingly problematized as incivility, whose opinions are not convincingly canvassed, whose participation is not convincingly sought, and whose mere presence is perceived as a threat to enterprise" (Neocleous, 2000, p. 398). Neocleous explains that security requires "the process of securing," which he describes as a commodity-based solution. He argues that to sell this commodity, the security industry must "play on existing fears and insecurities, must generate further fears and insecurities, must pander to the idea that our fears and insecurities are very real, and must peddle the belief that all insecurities need to be dealt with in some way" to sell products and services (p. 34). Therefore, there are deep financial interests behind defining perceptions of insecurity and safety.

Many scholars have argued that powerful financial interests have always been at the heart of surveillance-based solutions to community safety. In 1999, the Carnegie Community Action Project argued that CCTV cameras produced a specific way of visualizing the city, and criticized CCTV for aligning community goals with spaces that would produce the most prosperous environment for capitalism over people. Similarly, Coleman and Sim (2004) argue that CCTV surveillance stemmed from elite interests that sought to make the city appear as a safe place to do business, mirroring Amazon's influx of surveillance cameras on porches to make them safe places for parcels to be delivered. Coleman and Sim emphasize that the powerful discursive interventions of elite partnerships were central to the construction of risky bodies and the development of a local, social-ordering strategy. This strategy was facilitated by CCTV technology and used to define who should be targeted to avoid perceived risks and danger. They explained that the categories of people who were primarily constructed as suspicious and against the "public interest" of the city were centred around youth, homeless persons, street traders and Black men. By equating malign intent with appearances, CCTV operators have imposed "a 'normative space-time ecology' on the city by stipulating who 'belongs' where and when, and treating everything else as a suspicious 'other' to be disciplined, scrutinised, controlled" (Graham, 1998, p. 491).

Despite Ring having managed to brand the acts of watching and sharing content to be forms of collective action and empowerment, these are highly individuated acts that may harm actual community relationships. For example, Adam Crawford (1998) has questioned the effectiveness of the responsibilized policing public and whether communities can contribute to the construction of social order. He argues that "the notion of community collides with existing social fragmentation and the commodification of security, which may fuel exclusionary elements of community safety practice" (p. 237). One notable tension Crawford highlights is how appeals to community can collide with real social and spatial inequalities which "misunderstands and over-estimates the role and contribution of communities in the construction of social order and the prevention of crime" (p. 238).

Steve Herbert (2005) complements Crawford's work by providing qualitative data to support this misrecognition of the role communities can play through informal policing systems such as Ring. Interviewing residents in Seattle neighbourhoods, Herbert found that residents do not envision a robust political role for community and that they do not feel powerful enough to enact meaningful policing, nor do they wish to play a policing role (Herbert, 2005). Herbert concludes that community can "give way" under the expectations that neoliberalism wishes to place upon it. This notion of community "giving way" echoes Neocleous's characterization of the fracturing within what he calls "homo securitas," the neoliberal, entrepreneurial subject oriented around security (2000). Neocleous (2005) argues that homo securitas is fractured through the simultaneous suspicion of the behaviour of others, the power to report them and the reflexive acknowledgement that they too are subject to other people's watching and reporting. He maintains that "we are all in both categories, constantly reminded that in this social order, we are meant to treat each other as the source of insecurity rather than solidarity or friendship" (2005, p. 39). Collective action in the form of online policing thus produces one way that community can give way under the corporate logic of neoliberalism, where social relationships are oriented around mutual insecurity and fear, rather than trust and solidarity.

CASE EXAMPLE III: CARE COLLECTIVES

Continuing with the themes of collectivity, empowerment and autonomy, the third case study highlights how the collective action that Mad/Disabled communities take toward meeting their care needs can be co-opted by neoliberal governments or influenced by wider neoliberal narratives. First, this case study examines the administration of user-directed programs, such as Ontario's Direct Funding program, before going on to consider the ways neoliberal narratives shape the organizing of Mad/Disabled support networks.

Community care and Disability Rights narratives of autonomy and choice have resulted in shifts in the way that institutional care is administered, leading to the development of programs, such as Ontario's Direct Funding model. Hande and Kelly (2015) have critiqued Ontario's Direct Funding program; they argue that it increases the responsibilization of individual service users to manage the administration of their own care through the development of user-centred services. Alongside a narrative of increased user choice and autonomy over care, user-administered services also support the shrinkage of government-administered care, which can create new administrative barriers to care — particularly for those unable to administer care for themselves. Similarly, within Mad/Disabled communities, participants from Morris's (2023) study noted the ways in which care in these communities tends to prioritize short-term emergency needs over long-term or ongoing care requirements. Drawing parallels between "episodic" and "crisis-centred" care and neoliberal concepts of "flexibility," this case example argues that even Mad/Disabled community networks are shaped by the logic of neoliberalism.

Mad/Disabled communities have been labelled by normative care institutions as in need of care and "unable" to care for themselves because of their varying ability, mental capacity or deviation from its normative — that is, able-bodied, neurotypical, productive — neoliberal subjectivity. The ways in which these communities have been labelled as "in need of care" have worked to justify coercive and non-consensual "care" practices, such as the forced sterilization and involuntary institutionalization of Disabled and neurodivergent people. For Disabled communities, in particular, care and caregiving can be a site of coercion, in the ways that this community can both lack autonomy in choosing the terms of care while also being dependent on the care provided by institutions (Eales & Peers, 2021). This history of "caring for" Disabled people has encouraged the movement toward user-directed care models, which allow Disabled people greater autonomy over their own care.

Access to care significantly impacts Mad/Disabled people and communities. Care institutions can both facilitate access to essential services or care for Mad/Disabled communities and have the power to remove services or deny access to care. Mad/Disabled interactions with care services and institutions thus influence health and life outcomes for these communities. Given this context, there has been an effort in Mad/Disabled communities to increase Mad/Disabled autonomy and choice in care.

Queer and disabled scholars have argued that institutional care is embedded within larger systems of oppression, state power and violence including ableism, colonialism, racism, white supremacy and eugenics (Clare, 2017; Eales & Peers, 2021; Piepzna-Samarasinha, 2018). As Leah Lakshmi Piepzna-Samarasinha reminds us, care is "complicated" (2018, p. 9) and always bound up with power. Institutionalization and care have been used as a tool of colonial expansion (Voronka, 2008) and to justify the involuntary and forced confinement of Indigenous people and those labelled mad, disabled, or otherwise, "in need of care" (Mackelprang & Salsgiver, 2022, p. 1). Given this history, caring for Mad and Disabled people has always been connected to eugenics. Eales and Peers write of the ways that, at its core, eugenics is "about care," where caring for the nation or the future becomes about the inclusion of some people and communities into the future and not others. Namely, it is those who are seen as different or diseased who are excluded from the ideal future under eugenics. As such, care is never neutral, and what we care for and what form that care takes, shapes the ways in which care becomes bound up with other systems of power.

As mentioned above, dominant discourses of care have been critiqued for situating Mad/Disabled people as in need of care. Being "cared for" or "taken into care" for Disabled communities is associated with institutionalization and confinement (Eales & Peers, 2021; Piepzna-Samarasinha, 2018; Mackelprang & Salsgiver, 2009). Within colonial contexts, care is a site of violence, coercion and control (Eales & Peers; Piepzna-Samarasinha). In the context of neoliberal state care, subjects are understood following reductive categories of capacity or debility, able-bodied or disabled (Puar, 2012). For those for whom debility and disability are ongoing, there are consequences across all spheres of social life under neoliberalism in terms of opportunity, health and life outcomes (Soldatic, 2020). For the ideal, neoliberal subject who is adaptable, self-sufficient, autonomous and labouring, disability and being "in need of care" is something to be avoided. As a form of population and crisis management, neoliberalism constructs a binary wherein one is either in total dependency and in need of care, or they are capable and independent.

Arguing that a "logic of ableism" is highly complementary to the guiding tenets of neoliberalism, Goodley and Lawthom (2019) use the term **neoliberal-ableism** to describe how neoliberalism and ableism are intertwined. These discourses interact to view each instance of crisis as an individual problem to be solved, assuming that each period of crisis is episodic in nature and that a return to normative able-bodied life post-crisis is possible. McRuer (2006) similarly introduces the late capitalist concept of "flexibility" as a requirement of neoliberal expansion, inequality and resource extraction where labour, production and practices are all "flexible, mobile, and replaceable" (p. 17). Flexibility allows neoliberal subjects to quickly respond to the ongoing periods of episodic crisis produced by late capitalism, flexibly responding to each condition of crisis before returning to normal, unchanged and prepared for the next crisis. It is through flexibility and returning to the norm that neoliberalism manages and contains crisis, as a series of seemingly separate problems to be mitigated, managed and contained.

Unlike institutional care — which for Mad/Disabled communities often fails to meet community care needs and which can also be a site of violence, coercion and control — community care by and for Mad/Disabled communities provides a collective alternative to accessing state care. Community care practices provide physical assistance or emotional support, creating interdependent and collaborative approaches to care while also building community, developing relationships and support networks and making life more livable. Care in these communities operates as a socially innovative form of collective action, which, like the other examples in this chapter, defines the borders of community.

The neoliberal-ableism of managing and mitigating each individual crisis before moving on to the next through short periods of crisis-specific response is reproduced in Mad/Disabled communities through emergency response webs. In Morris's (2023) study, participants noted how communities mobilize resources quickly when someone experiences sudden injury or illness. One participant described the "ableist expectation of getting better," and how support drops off as care needs become ongoing and one doesn't get better or return to "normal," non-disabled life. Queer of colour **crip** writers have also criticized the ways short-term care is prioritized over long-term care, particularly within activist and mutual aid circles (Arani, 2020; Piepzna-Samarasinha, 2018). In short-term emergency care models, communities respond to episodes of crisis, flexibly mobilizing around a specific need before returning to normal, as if the crisis had not occurred in the first place. Alongside the ways that Mad/Disabled community care mobilizations resist neoliberal discourses of ableism, neoliberal concepts of flexibility and episodic crisis continue to influence community care.

Community care as an alternative to state care operationalizes social relations within Mad/Disabled communities to meet care needs on a community level. As a collective approach to caring with each other and a community response to meeting individual care needs, care collectives transform individualizing, neoliberal systems of care into collective frameworks for care and respond to conditions of crisis by centring interdependent relationships. Participants in Morris's (2023) study describe a framework of mutual support in which reciprocity and mutual care take place in indirect ways. Following an understanding of interdependence that sees community care needs as interconnected with each other, reciprocity and care become extended through vast community networks, rather than following a dichotomous model of reciprocity based on mutual exchange and equal giving. One participant described mutual support as a practice of meeting community needs as they arise and "showing up for other people" when they need support. Rather than more direct forms of reciprocity, mutual support here is based on the trust that members support each other as a collective. Extending practices of care to a wider community without the expectation of receiving direct reciprocity in return reconfigures social relationships around care to emphasize a process-oriented approach to collectively addressing community needs.

Institutional care and broader neoliberal discourses of care also have impacts on the ways Mad/Disabled communities mobilize in response to care needs. For example, participants described situations where short-term emergency care was prioritized over ongoing care needs within care collectives, following the neoliberal principles of scarcity and episodic crisis. Alongside reconfiguring social relations to centre community care needs, community care practices are also shaped by wider neoliberal discourses of scarcity and crisis that motivate communities to prioritize short-term emergency care over long-term and ongoing forms of care.

76 INTERRUPTING INNOVATION

Beyond operationalizing social relations within Mad/Disabled communities to meet collective care needs, care collectives (and other community mobilizations around care) transform Mad/Disabled communities' relationships to care institutions and the way care is administered. In the mid-twentieth century, Mad and Disabled people began organizing together in response to the conditions they experienced in care services, including their right to receive state care and social recognition. The Disability Rights Movement followed a "minority model of disability," that argued that Disabled people are minorities, and, as minorities, are subjected to discrimination and a lack of opportunity; and that it is these social barriers, and not individual characteristics or disabilities, that were the greatest barrier to Disabled people's full participation in society (Mackelprang & Salsgiver, 2009). Unlike other identity groups seeking equality, Disabled people are often in the unique position of needing care, or otherwise being "dependent" on the state, making possible disability-specific kinds of abuse and harm within institutional care settings. Given this history of institutional care, the Disability Rights Movement sought to increase Mad/Disabled autonomy over their care.

The Disability Rights Movement also led to the development of more user-directed approaches to administering care. Disability activists argued they were denied rights to education and employment based on their disabilities, and their demands for civil rights brought forth programs such as the Independent Living Movement (Mackelprang & Salsgiver, 2009). In Canada, the Disability Rights Movement also led to the development of user-directed publicly funded programs, such as Ontario's Direct Funding program, as noted earlier (Hande & Kelly, 2015). However, these advancements also work against notions of interdependence and community-based care. While Direct Funding gives Disabled people agency over their own care, it also responsibilizes Disabled people in administering their own care, resulting in different challenges for service users. Hande and Kelly (2015) have noted the ways that, alongside its many benefits to service users and increased autonomy over the terms of care, Direct Funding can also be connected to neoliberalism through the self-responsibilization of service users. Similar to the narrative of empowerment used by Amazon Ring to encourage users to adopt surveillance technology in order to participate in their own safety and risk management, Direct Funding also self-responsibilizes service users who are encouraged to self-administer their own care using an empowerment narrative. While this narrative of empowerment resulted in increased choice and autonomy over care, it has also been incorporated into institutional care frameworks to justify the shrinking of government-administered care services alongside the responsibilization of service users following a narrative of "autonomy" and "choice."

Direct Funding and Amazon Ring, as two different examples of transformative social innovation that rely on an empowerment narrative to encourage users to adopt services, both resulted in changes in the ways service users interact with institutions in ways that are not necessarily positive. In the case of Direct Funding, the expansion of this program increases the self-administration of care services, supporting the ongoing shrinkage of government-administered care services by using a narrative of increased choice. Direct Funding is an example of one of the ways a socially innovative practice can be co-opted by external actors and lead to widespread institutional changes, which challenges the assumption that social innovation is desirable and leads to social benefit.

CONCLUSION

In these three case examples, communities mobilize around socially innovative practices that seek to operationalize social relationships and transform institutions. As disparate forms of collective action, the narratives and strategies circulated by misogynist incel forums, the surveillance technology of Amazon Ring and the collective care practices of Mad/Disabled communities all seek to respond to, or otherwise shape, the distribution of life chances of a specific community. These examples point to the application of social innovation as a framework to identify divergent social responses to larger structural conditions — in this case, the conditions of neoliberalism and late capitalism. Rather than being inherently, socially progressive, social innovation can take on a variety of divergent forms, transforming social relations to achieve a social goal.

In the first example, incels were defined by their experiences of social alienation: beyond a lack of romantic or sexual connection with others, they often entirely lack care networks. Exploring their networked discourses illustrates how incels seek to change the terms of social relations to address this real or perceived need. Their attempts to manifest care for themselves or their community might travel down two paths — lay down or lash out. These responses revolve around care: to isolate oneself from possibilities for care and connection on purpose; to avoid the expected disappointment of rejection; or to punish others for seeming not to care about incel "suffering, and thus to seek redress for "harms" perpetrated against them. These transformative strategies are manifestly negative, with tragic and brutal consequences for all parties. This example illustrates how efforts to change social relations to serve community goals can be reactionary just as often as they can be progressive.

In the second case example, we examined Amazon Ring as a socially innovative tool, as well as an agent steering social innovation. The case study took up the dialectical nature of empowerment, wherein social innovation can be both empowering and disempowering. Ring can be seen as empowering by enabling users to see who is at their door prior to answering it to avoid unwanted interactions; and disempowering by reducing community interaction and care to pre-defined, online actions. We examined ways that Ring is changing social relations and whether the counter-effects of this social innovation are ones we want to solidify as infrastructure and carry into the future.

The third case example discussed how despite the intentions of collective, community care practices (a socially innovative practice), there is always the risk that external actors can co-opt a movement or narrative to benefit themselves personally or to uphold the status quo. In the case of Direct Funding, the need for autonomy and choice in care has been used both to develop a program that grants qualifying Disabled people increased choice and control over the way their care is administered, while also responsibilizing service users for their own care and placing limits on who is able to access care services. This raises important questions about who is empowered to make decisions about their care, and how this influences the distribution of resources across Disabled communities. Disabled people who are better resourced are more likely to have higher levels of cognitive capacity and more predictable, stable care needs and therefore are more likely to benefit from Direct Funding.

As pointed out by Leah Lakshmi Piepzna-Samarasinha (2018), in the case of informal community care practices, those who are well-liked, have more friends, have better access to resources, have the ability to provide care to others, are good at articulating and communicating their care needs and whose care needs are more easily managed may receive higher quality care from their community. Even in considering transformative social movements that lead to significant changes in the ways communities relate to one another or work to meet a given need, one must keep in mind the uneven ways in which empowerment plays out, particularly along gendered, racialized and class lines. In sum, communities innovate toward social change in myriad ways, and innovation by itself should not necessarily be read as progressive and positive. Rather, the roots of community-driven innovation need to be examined using social innovation theory to better understand the power dynamics and stakes at play in the innovation process.

Reflection Questions

1. Pick one of the case examples and discuss how social innovation can have unintended consequences that can harm community. Undertake a similar reflection on an example from your own experience or area of practice.
2. Can you think of an example of an empowerment narrative? How might it be (or has it been) co-opted by an external actor for their own usage?

REFERENCES

Ankel, S. (2020). A 23-year-old man accidentally blew his hands off after planning an incel attack on a shopping mall, say FBI. *Business Insider.* businessinsider.com.au/virginia-man-planned-incel-attack-accidentally- blows-his-hands-off-2020-6

Arani, A. (2020). Mutual aid and its ambivalences: Lessons from sick and disabled trans and Queer people of color. *Feminist Studies, 46*(3), 653–622.

Avelino, F., Wittmayer, J.M., Pel, B., Weaver, P., Dumitru, A., et al. (2019). Transformative social innovation and (dis)empowerment. *Technological Forecasting & Social Change, 145,* 195–206.

BBC. (2018, April 25). Elliot Rodger: *How misogynist killer became "incel hero." BBC.* bbc.com/news/world-us-canada-43892189

BBC. (2020, May 20). *Teenage boy charged in Canada's first "incel" terror case. BBC.* bbc.com/news/world-us-canada-52733060

Brockbank, N. (2019, September 27). Alek Minassian reveals details of Toronto van attack in video of police interview. *CBC News.* cbc.ca/news/canada/toronto/alek-minassian-police-interview-1.5298021

Carnegie Community Action Project. (1999, July). *Closed Circuit Television: Surveillance of public space in Vancouver.* Carnegie Community Action Project. chodarr.org/sites/default/files/chodarr0331.pdf.

CBC News. (2019, January 27). Why incels are a "real and present threat" for Canadians. *CBC News.* cbc.ca/news/canada/incel-threat-canadians-fifth-estate-1.4992184

CBC Radio Canada. (2018, April 25). How the misogynistic, insular world of "incels" may have inspired the Toronto van attack. *CBC News.* cbc.ca/news/canada/toronto/what-is-an-incel-toronto-van-attack-explainer- alek-minassian-1.4633893

Clare, E. (2017). *Brilliant imperfection: Grappling with cure.* Duke University Press.

Coleman, & Sim, J. (2000). 'You'll never walk alone': CCTV surveillance, order and neo-liberal rule in Liverpool city centre. *The British Journal of Sociology, 51*(4), 623–639.

Cottee, S. (2020). Incel (e) motives: Resentment, shame and revenge. *Studies in Conflict & Terrorism, 44*(2), 93–114.

Crary, J. (2013). *24/7: Late capitalism and the ends of sleep.* Verso.

Crawford, A. (1998). Community safety and the quest for security: Holding back the dynamics of social exclusion. *Policy Studies, 19*(3-4), 237–253.

Eales, L., & Peers, D. (2021). Care haunts, hurts, heals: The promiscuous poetics of queer crip Mad care. *Journal of Lesbian Studies, 25*(3), 163–181.

Fougere, M., & Merilainen, E. (2021). Exposing three dark sides of social innovation through critical perspectives on resilience. *Industry and Innovation, 28*(1), 1–18.

Gilling, D. (2001). Community safety and social policy. *European Journal on Criminal Policy and Research, 9*(4), 381–400.

80 INTERRUPTING INNOVATION

Goodley, D., & Lawthom, R. (2019). Critical disability studies, Brexit and Trump: A time of neoliberal-ableism. *Rethinking History, 23*(2), 233–251.

Graham, S. (1998). Spaces of surveillant simulation: New technologies, digital representations, and material geographies. *Environment and Planning D: Society and Space, 16*(4), 483–504.

Hande, M. J., & Kelly, C. (2015). Organizing survival and resistance in austere times: Shifting disability activism and care politics in Ontario, Canada. *Disability & Society, 30*(7), 961-975.

Hermer, J., Kempa, M., Shearing, C., Stenning, P., & Wood, J. (2005). Policing in Canada in the twenty-first century: Directions for law reform. In D. Cooley (Ed.), *Re-imagining policing in Canada* (pp. 22-91). University of Toronto Press.

Hoffman, B., Ware, J., & Shapiro, E. (2020). Assessing the threat of incel violence. *Studies in Conflict & Terrorism, 43*(7), 565–587.

Kelly, M., DiBranco, A., & DeCook, J.R. (2021, February 18). Misogynist incels and male supremacism: Overview and recommendations for addressing the threat of male supremacist violence. *New America, Institute for Research on Male Supremacism.* newamerica.org/political-reform/reports/misogynist-incels-and-male- supremacism/

Kimmel, M. S. (2013). *Angry white men: American masculinity at the end of an era.* Nation Books.

Lakshmi Piepzna-Samarasinha, L. (2018). *Care work: Dreaming disability justice.* Arsenal Pulp Press.

Mackelprang, R. W., & Salsgiver, R. O. (2009). *Disability: A diversity model approach in human service practice* (2nd ed.). Lyceum Books.

Marwick. (2013). *Status update: Celebrity, publicity, and branding in the social media age.* Yale University Press.

McChesney, R. W. (1999). Noam Chomsky and the struggle against neoliberalism. *Monthly Review, 50*(4), 40–47.

McRuer, R. (2006). *Crip theory: Cultural signs of queerness and disability.* New York University Press.

Morris, L. (2023). *Cultivating community care: Using research-creation & art-based workshops to explore care in queer and mad/disabled communities in Toronto.* [Master's Thesis, Toronto Metropolitan University and York University]. Toronto Metropolitan University Library e-Reserve.

Neocleous, M. (2021). *A critical theory of police power: The fabrication of the social order.* Verso.

Nishida, A. (2016). Neoliberal academia and a critique from disability studies. In P. Block, D. Kasnitz, A. Nishida, & N. Pollard (Eds.), *Occupying disability: Critical approaches to community, justice, and decolonizing disability* (pp. 145-157). Springer.

Puar, J. K. (2012). Coda: The cost of getting better—suicide, sensation, switchpoints. *GLQ, 18*(1), 149–158.

Soldatic, K. (2020). Social suffering in the neoliberal age: Surplusity and the partially disabled subject. In N. Watson, & S. Vehmas (Eds.), *Routledge handbook of disability studies* (pp. 237-249). Routledge.

Thuy Vo, L. (2022, August 25). Porch piracy: Are we overreacting to package thefts from doorsteps? *The Guardian.* theguardian.com/us-news/2022/aug/25/porch-piracy-package-thefts-doorstep-delivery

Voronka, J. (2008). Re/moving forward? Spacing mad degeneracy at the Queen Street site. *Resources for Feminist Research, 33*(1/2), 45–61.

Witt, T. (2020). "If I cannot have it, I will do everything I can to destroy it.": The canonization of Elliot Rodger: "Incel" masculinities, secular sainthood, and justifications of ideological violence. *Social Identities, 26*(5), 675–689.

Power Sharing, Community Leadership and Dynamic Governance at the SHIFT Centre for Social Transformation

SHIFT Governance Hub Members
Cheryl Gladu, Stephanie Childs, Kristen Young and Katarina Prystay

> **Learning Objectives**
> 1. Explain the relationship between organizational design, sharing power, innovation, and justice.
> 2. Understand the relationship between organizational design and organizational effectiveness in the context of social innovation.
> 3. Recognize some of the design features of dynamic systems of governance and the principles that help them work sustainably.

THE SHIFT CENTRE FOR SOCIAL TRANSFORMATION (SHIFT) has become the unlikely but welcoming home for an experiment in collaborative governance of a multi-million-dollar, open-ended social change project hosted at Concordia University in Montreal, Canada. Founded in 2019, its focus is to support existing and emerging initiatives that work for systemic change in Montreal on issues of justice, equity and sustainability. Its governance system is designed to centre marginalized perspectives in decision-making about resource allocation.

During the pandemic, when Zoom fatigue had settled in, we opened the SHIFT steering committee (SC) meeting with a reach for creativity: "On the screen, you'll see an image of a diverse ecosystem — the birds soaring above, the buffalo tearing up prairie grasses with their hooves, the mycelium under the soil reaching across root systems, transferring nutrients throughout the system. Imagine this is the SHIFT ecosystem. Which element of the ecosystem represents the role that you play?" A year later, a member of the SC, Nafija, states: "I still remember that check-in question. I am the lichen!" she says. "I am the lichen growing on the rock, and I am so strong to be able to grow there. At SHIFT, the lichen is as beautiful as the fox. That is what is so special here."

82 INTERRUPTING INNOVATION

Nafija is one of the two dozen community members involved in this experiment of collaborative governance. A self-described "community unifier," Nafija is a board member of one of SHIFT's funded projects, works as a Bangla-English-French interpreter in the health and justice system and has sat on SHIFT's SC since 2019. Her description of SHIFT as a place where "the lichen is as beautiful as the fox" is a telling metaphor for the deeper purpose of SHIFT — a gesture toward a place within an institution where it becomes possible to feel into the potentials of the pluriverse, a world where many worlds fit (Escobar, 2018).

By way of a case study, we invite the reader to consider the role of organizational design in creating and maintaining social innovation initiatives. The example of SHIFT illustrates how embedding policies and practices for sharing power can act as a safeguard against losing focus on social justice outcomes, and thus the socially transformative potential of social innovation spaces. Anchoring our work in social transformation calls us to bring forward experiments that engage with the explicit (policies, practices and resource flows), semi-implicit (relationships and power dynamics) and implicit (mental models) frameworks that maintain systems of injustice (Kania, Kramer, & Senge, 2018).

These experiments weave throughout the SHIFT ecosystem: as we bring together people of different backgrounds, disciplines and perspectives to understand complex, system-level issues and work efficiently and effectively to address them justly, we actively explore how power is held, and by whom. Knowing how we design organizations is important to ensure that we are not unintentionally recreating the systems we seek to contest. As we saw in Chapter 2 and Chapter 4, social innovation can have unintended, negative consequences that reproduce the status quo. Creating intentional organizational space allows for thoughtful consideration of how to create community within the confines of institutional systems that may be resistant to reconfiguration of power dynamics. SHIFT offers a concrete example of how this intentional design, based on social innovation thinking, can provide and safeguard space for transformation, even within institutional settings where power sharing in governance may not be the norm.

This chapter opens with a theoretical overview of the connection between organizational design and innovation writ large, describing the concept of dynamic systems of governance, and briefly reviews a model for dynamic governance that has inspired our work — namely Sociocracy. We then delve into the case of SHIFT's governance model and the role it has had in effecting and embodying social transformation, including a first-person account of the experience of engaging with this model. This case demonstrates how governance, by way of organizational design, provides the frame through which the principles and practices of power-sharing can be woven into an organizational fabric.

There is radical potential for social change in enabling community groups closest to the issues at hand to leverage philanthropic and institutional resources and knowledge in pursuit of their visions for transformation. This contrasts with traditional, hierarchical models of governance, where power over decision-making flows from top to bottom, which persists in areas of philanthropic activity, as well as within the broader social innovation sector. In detailing SHIFT's unique approach to governance, its principles and practices, we see the potential for other social innovation organizations to learn and adopt structures for power-sharing in their governance and meaningfully imbue the communities at the heart of their practice with power over their transformation.

BACKGROUND AND CONTEXT

Given the broad nature of the framing of social innovation and the potential for us to conflate different approaches to similar goals, thought has gone into the distinctions that can be made when we consider both the nature of the action that an organization takes in pursuit of positive, social and environmental change (direct vs. indirect), and whether the outcome of those actions simply improve the existing system/context or facilitates the emergence of a new, sustainable equilibrium (Martin, Roger, & Osberg, 2007). We are mostly considering the work of organizations that take direct action with the intention of developing an enduring, transformational benefit to society. We know too that disruptive forms of innovation often arise from the edges — for instance, where smaller organizations with few resources can successfully challenge established ways of doing in plain sight of established actors (Christensen, Raynor, & McDonald, 2015). For this reason, it's important to pay attention to and learn from the cases that are challenging norms and consider not just how they are different or difficult, but to appreciate how they can be both daring and desirable for more people.

It is worth stressing that as we consider a pathway to addressing these complex problems via social innovation, we don't lose sight of the centrality of what we are doing together to address such problems, and how we are doing this — preferably in a way that doesn't reproduce the logic that has led to our current struggles (Jimenez et al., 2022; Lefebvre, 1976). One of the more important challenges for social progress of any kind is the redesign of the cultural underpinnings that have since guided us astray, as such structures shape our habits of interaction (Ehrenfeld, 2009). Just as social innovation has gained some prominence in literature, so has an interest in governance, with something of a systemic turn toward deliberative processes and participative practices (e.g., Bjorgvinsson, Ehn, & Hillgren, 2012; Ercan & Dryzek, 2015; Felicetti, 2018). As has been observed, neither the state nor the market is uniformly successful in enabling people to share resources in a long-term, sustainable manner, yet there are many examples of communities of people who have developed reliable institutions that do not resemble state or market actors, and many of these have had reasonable degrees of success over long periods in managing shared resources; these organizations are self-governed (Ostrom, 1990).

The central role that work plays in the daily lives of citizens, be that in the private, public or non-governmental organizational sectors, has led to reflections on the role of unelected power within democratic societies in such places (Felicetti, 2018), and popular discourse presents the notion that many of the main challenges faced by contemporary society are routed in the disproportionate power wielded by the few at the top of larger organizations (Klein, 2015; Taibbi, 2014). Further, as we pursue sustainable development of the deepest and most resilient sort, we must consider what it might look like to close the gaps in welfare, health and justice that exist between those in and out of power. One way to enable this move toward a more equitable society is through the development and testing of more democratic forms of governance, which enable more citizen participation in the decisions that affect their everyday lives (Ehn, Nilsson, & Topgaard, 2014). There is a very real sense that organizational governance may have a role in fostering responsible conduct (Ostrom, 1990; Romme, 2003) and innovation (Daft, Murphy, & Willmott, 2020; Manz, Shipper, & Stewart, 2009; Semler, 1989).

The paradox of organizational design is that, on its own, it is rather empty; it accomplishes nothing without the people and the actions they take together. Yet at the same time, it can have the effect of creating a central framing for people's outlooks and interpretations of what is going on around them, leading to "the social construction of rules and relationships — through which structure is enacted" (Bate, Khan, & Pye, 2000, p. 200). It is perhaps this paradox that leads organizational design to be something of a troublesome afterthought in the creation of many organizations, but most worryingly so in the case of social impact organizations. Many fall into habits of formal leadership and these structures shape our relationships, especially as an organization scales up in size or impact, wherein there exists a perennial threat of increased centralization of power in the hands of a minority elite (Diefenbach, 2019). In a context of continuous and tumultuous change, it's not enough for formal leaders to be learned and adaptable; the whole organization must be constructed to learn and adapt. This is especially true in the case of the formation of mission-driven organizations. Organizations that stand the greatest chance of sustainability and address such concerns will be those that are both locally and culturally responsive. What better way to be responsive than to be led from the ground up?

BRIEF INTRODUCTION TO ORGANIZATIONAL THEORY AND DESIGN

From trade guilds, unions and merchant associations and into the formal emergence of the legal, cooperative movement in the nineteenth century, people have long been organizing to address injustices and to better their collective position through cooperation. This is a history full of starts, stops and overlapping narratives of average people seeking to participate more fully in the decisions that affect their lives. In the late twentieth century, organizational theorists and practitioners recognized the role of organizational design in the need for more accountability and transparency in the organizations that purport to serve us. Initially, this took the form of corporate governance reforms meant to include shareholders (vs. employees or other stakeholders) in decision-making via mechanisms like annual general meetings. It later expanded to include stakeholders who potentially held some political power over the organization, such as local officials or other community representatives. Modern stakeholder theory advocates for considering the interests of all stakeholders, including employees, customers and the community. In moving beyond approaches of mere engagement, we must consider direct and meaningful approaches to co-governance or power sharing.

Several emergent models of organizational design are grounded in the notion that management can — and should — be led by the employees or members of the organization. This approach is often called self-governance or self-management. In such a context, traditional managerial functions (such as planning, organizing, staffing and controlling) are shared among employees (Daft, Murphy, & Willmott, 2020). While there is plenty to be managed, there are no managers per se. There is plenty of leadership, but an absence of the kind of formal authority that accompanies a leadership position. Leadership is more of a process than a particular person (Raelin, 2014).

The organizational design turn toward self-management reflects a fundamental shift in the way we conceive of organizational models and asks theorists and practitioners alike to move beyond increasingly popular concepts, such as employee empowerment and engagement; distributed decision-making; and flatter organizations writ large (Daft, Murphy, & Willmott, 2020; Denis, Lamothe, & Langley, 2001; Raelin, 2014). Complete self-management can include these ideas, and others still, as it incorporates the notion that employees or members of an organization can and should participate in the emergence of the nature of the organization — not just in the activities that transpire on the day-to-day, but also in the development and evolution of its mission and vision. Self-governance is meaningful because it is fundamentally about changing the power relations present in organizations, thereby allowing participants to "negate the existing, to de-construct or 'de-structure' it in order to reconstruct it, radically transformed" (Lefebvre 1976, p. 81).

Like other human systems, these approaches to governance have been co-evolving with less democratic governance structures, but have only recently appeared in the literature around organizational design (Lee & Edmondson, 2017; Romme & Van Witteloostuijn, 1999; Manz, Shipper, & Stewart, 2009; Semler, 1989) double and triple loop learning. There are an increasing number of tested approaches to enabling self-governance, many of them evolving and responsive to the local context and organizational mission. This dynamism and adaptability have led to a number of these organizational designs to be described as "dynamic" systems of governance (Romme & Van Witteloostuijn, 1999), as they not only have this novel quality of self-management, but a resulting nimbleness that is also associated with innovation — including social innovation.

We will briefly consider one model, Sociocracy, that is both studied and well-understood for illustration, and has a connection to SHIFT as our case model. The Sociocratic model is grounded in Quaker concepts of equality and leaderless governance, and it emphasizes the use of collective reasoning rather than voting per se (Boeke, 1945). The Sociocratic model adopted by organizations today was formalized by Dutch entrepreneur Gerard Endenburg (Romme, 2003; Romme & Endenburg, 2006)

In this model, decisions are reached once a proposal overcomes any objections to its advancement (Buck & Villines, 2007). Since this time, Sociocracy has been adopted successfully by numerous organizations looking to create more deliberative and humane places to live and work.

The central objective of Sociocracy is to bolster the organization's ability to govern, structure and learn autonomously (Romme et al., 2016). Acknowledging the intricate, dynamic nature of organizational structures that evolve through dialectical interactions (Raelin, 2014), decision-making unfolds hierarchically at various levels within the organization through organizational groups or circles which employ informed consent as a decision-making mechanism. Given the connectedness among these circles of governance, ideas are better able to circulate from the operational levels up to the strategic levels of the organization. This dynamic design streamlines informed consent across all levels, minimizing the need for frequent plenary discussions, and enabling groups to delegate day-to-day decision-making to smaller teams operating at the most relevant level (Romme & Endenburg, 2006).

Informed consent is fostered by providing participants with the opportunity to express and discuss objections to a proposal in advance of its progression, within more manageable settings, including smaller teams (Romme, 2004). This decision-making approach aims to establish a formal space for the comprehensive communication and exploration of dissenting perspectives within the group. Essentially, the process encourages the identification and proactive addressing of challenging issues by creating a framework for surfacing tensions and facilitating their resolution (Gladu, Paquin, & Prakash, 2020) at the level of the organization where it will have the largest and most direct impact. Those who are impacted by the rules play an active role in shaping them.

It is worth noting that decision-making in such a context is not without challenges. Ospina and Saz-Carranza (2010) describe these conditions as paradoxical, favouring both collaboration and confrontation. As diverse members deliberate, they are forced to generate new shared understanding (Isaacs 1999; 2001), knowledge (Tsoukas, 2009) and innovative pathways forward (Follett, 1925; Shipper, Manz, & Stewart, 2014). This can be achieved through the constructive resolution of issues (Gladu, Paquin, & Prakash, 2020; Isaacs, 2001; Tsoukas, 2009) or by respectfully agreeing to disagree (Mouffe, 1999), all of which are helpful approaches that contribute to a deepening understanding and may contribute to the development of skills needed to engage in civil discourse.

The challenges that may emerge from such organizational designs ultimately have the potential to be productive and effective from the standpoint of innovation. As we will see in the case below, struggle is an essential characteristic of both the process of trying to understand the root causes of complex issues and is a central feature of truly participatory processes. The deliberation that is central to seeking consent in a diverse context can act as a catalyst for exploring alternatives and acting as a foundational element for initiating real social change (Brand, 2020). Such dynamic governance frameworks are an important tool for formalizing community leadership and accountability to stakeholders within social innovation spaces; they also serve as a foundation for developing a culture of community ownership, community care and deep valuing of diverse perspectives. Structures that share power need to be a feature of the designs of social innovation organizations for them to maintain their radical potential. Dynamic governance allows us to do the above.

THE SHIFT CENTRE FOR SOCIAL TRANSFORMATION

SHIFT is a unique experiment in leveraging institutional resources, knowledge and capacities toward social impact through deep, respectful and mutually beneficial relationships with community partners, organizations and grassroots initiatives. We use the example of SHIFT to illustrate what shared power and dynamic governance concretely look like in practice. Since its inauguration in 2019, SHIFT has supported and accompanied over fifty organizations and teams that share the objective of creating a more just, inclusive and broadly prosperous city. SHIFT offers funding, learning opportunities, capacity-building resources and access to physical space to teams tackling systemic issues, while offering tangible support to the communities most affected by them. Supported projects range widely in areas of focus, from the waste crisis to Indigenous food sovereignty (a complete list of such projects can be found at "Funded Partners–Concordia University," n.d.).

SHIFT emerged from a long history of community-engaged research, teaching and student organizing at Concordia University. Faculty members across campus were convened to ground the prospective initiative in Concordia's existing network of relationships. This inaugural, multidisciplinary steering committee (SC) — composed of activists, community-engaged artists, academics, engineers, students and community leaders — was responsible for articulating SHIFT's founding principles, including its vision, mission and values under the umbrella of social transformation:

> Social Transformation is an intentional process of systemic change to address not only the symptoms but the root causes of inequity, injustice and unsustainability. A project that has a transformative social impact is one that brings about change at the level of a whole system — impacting social norms and beliefs, resource consumption patterns, rules and practices, technologies and infrastructures, and/or the distribution of power.

Insomuch as social innovation is an approach to solutions-finding whereby the value created accrues primarily to society, this transformational lens facilitates social innovation that goes beyond the provision of social services toward actions that may lead to novel, systems-level disruptions. Activities are focused on supporting selected project teams in achieving their next level of impact, with community leadership and shared decision-making as central organizing principles over its structure and resources ("Programs–Concordia University," n.d.).

SHIFT's funding programs provide financial backing for established and emergent socially transformative initiatives in the Montreal area. Beyond the financial support received, these projects are also integrated into the vibrant SHIFT Learning Community, gaining access to an array of additional non-financial support. All of SHIFT's funding decisions are made by independent, selection juries, composed of a diverse group of community members and partners. Jury members receive training from SHIFT, review applications independently and assess them for their alignment with selection criteria; they follow a structured and facilitated consent-based decision-making process to decide which projects will enter the SHIFT community and receive funding and support.

In addition to providing funding, SHIFT provides opportunities to learn about social transformation. Through events, trainings, workshop series and peer mentorship opportunities (see "Events–Concordia University," n.d.), members of community groups are encouraged to share ideas and experiences and to participate in governance to strengthen their mutual goals of social change.

Further, SHIFT acts as the convenor and liaison of a large, rich network of connections — the SHIFT ecosystem. We accompany project teams in engaging with members of this network to expand their impact, through partnerships at the university and across Montreal. Lateral convening opportunities bring groups together to strengthen movements and share successful practices; vertical convening programming supports grassroots organizers to collaborate or advocate with powerholders at institutions to work toward justice and equity. One way that SHIFT facilitates enriched connection opportunities is via the SHIFT Internship Program, whereby project teams identify roles they would like filled in their organizations and SHIFT assumes full financial and administrative responsibility for the placements of Concordia students in those roles.

Finally, SHIFT provides a collaborative, in-person workspace. Space for meeting, working and holding events is often at a premium in the community and on a university campus, so an important component of SHIFT's work is to operate a vibrant and welcoming space at the heart of the Concordia downtown campus with street-level visibility. Our strong commitment to community co-ownership is embedded into the management of the space, where partners, students and members of the SHIFT community are encouraged to meet, learn and work together at its campus location.

How SHIFT is organized and governed

SHIFT's commitment to being an externally responsive space that welcomes collaboration and shared decision-making from the community meant that community leadership was a central consideration of its structural design. SHIFT's governance model aims to achieve four main objectives ("Governance–Concordia University," n.d.):

1. Accountability to SHIFT stakeholder groups: Major decisions about SHIFT's resources must be informed by the diversity of perspectives that make up the SHIFT community.
2. Stewardship informed by a diversity of perspectives: To reduce structural gaps in how we understand our work and choose to move forward to actualize our vision, the mission, vision and values of SHIFT are held in collectivity.
3. Shared power as a tool for community engagement: The invitation to be meaningfully involved in decision-making is an engagement tool to build a community of people who feel engaged in and committed to realizing SHIFT's mission and vision.
4. SHIFT as a "socially transformative initiative" itself: Experiment with and contribute to collective learning about how different decision-making systems and shared power structures can contribute to systemic social change.

It was paramount to enable diverse stakeholders to voice their perspectives, and for SHIFT to be held accountable to them. This has been instrumental in fostering a vibrant ecosystem dedicated to bringing about systemic change in the broader Montreal community.

SHIFT pursues the above goals via a series of interrelating circles that connect via the steering committee, program hubs and staff circles (see Figure 12), which allows members from within and beyond the university to participate in various, impactful decision-making processes, from distributing funds to strategic planning. Importantly, strategic decisions are largely the responsibility of diverse committees that bring multiple perspectives to monthly meetings where decisions affecting core organizational outcomes are made. Staff members, deeply embedded in daily activities, are accountable for operational decisions. Liaison members, those who sit in multiple circles, enable information to flow between circles.

The SC is responsible for high-level organizational decisions, setting overall strategic priorities for future directions and overseeing resource allocation in line with SHIFT's mission, vision, values and ways of working. Annually, the SC reviews the previous year's activities, before deciding about SHIFT's upcoming strategic orientation. Members include Concordia faculty and students, members of SHIFT-funded project teams and people engaged in socially transformative work across Concordia and Montreal.

At the time of writing, SHIFT had four program hubs, each responsible for setting program-level orientations related to a specific area of SHIFT's work: fund disbursement; collaborative space; ecosystem activation; and participatory governance. These circles each have four to five members who meet monthly to consider the specifics of their respective program areas. Hub members are selected to bring together people with expertise related to the topic at hand, as well as those who are directly affected by the decisions made at that level of the organization. Each hub includes several links to other parts of the organization to enable coordination and information to flow between circles: one SC member, along with a staff member who is the lead on the program area. Anyone can be nominated or apply to become a member of a hub or the SC. A selection committee composed of people from across SHIFT's community is convened to review and select new members based on their applications, as well as on particular criteria, skills or perspectives that might be lacking in the current membership.

The core staff team functions with a five-member team of coordinators and is structured horizontally. Rather than having a director, such leadership functions are divided among this team; each takes the lead in specific domains, such as external representation, human resource management and partnership development. The staff team interfaces with the larger university community via support from Concordia's Senior Director of Community Engagement and Social Impact, who acts as the chair of the SC. SHIFT's work is also supported by a part-time administrative assistant and several part-time and student employees.

Each staff member is responsible for program development, execution and evaluation of their program areas, honouring the need for autonomy and creativity in their role. However, they also function within the supportive structure of a program team, offering them accompaniment via the work of a colleague in a supportive role. The staff member receives support from the program team in the form of troubleshooting, brainstorming, managerial, administrative or operational support, as needed. Questions of strategic importance concerning the program area are brought to the program hub for decision-making. This formal structure acts as the enabling architecture that supports shared power to flourish at SHIFT. Along with a commitment to consent-based decision-making at all levels, this structure allows the organization to benefit from having insight from a diverse range of experiences and to ensure that resource distribution and program development meet the needs of community members.

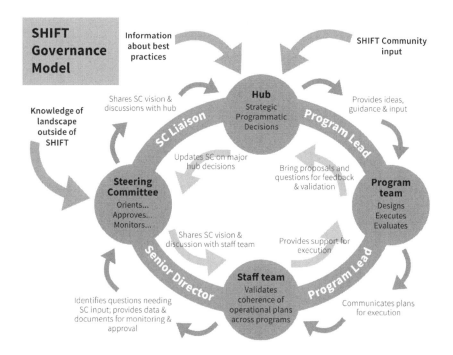

Figure 12: SHIFT Governance Model

PRINCIPLES AND PRACTICES THAT GUIDE THE WORK AT SHIFT

In addition to the formal structures outlined above are a series of principles and practices that guide informal relations between members of the organization.

Principle one: Cultivating meaningful diversity

Just as within a vibrant and thriving ecosystem in the natural world, diversity is critical to the composition of our decision-making circles. We aim to cultivate what we refer to as meaningful diversity, which means the individuals around the table bring different perspectives and types of expertise on the issue at hand, based on their different positionalities in relation to the subject. Particularly in relation to the issues of social transformation that are at the heart of SHIFT's work, members' perspectives are informed by the structural and systemic power to which they, as individuals, have access.

For instance, the Fund Disbursement Hub is responsible for setting the program-level strategy regarding SHIFT's funding programs. As such, it includes in its membership people with different experiences of **structural power** in relation to project funding. Some members contribute experience acquired through developing and executing programming in more traditional philanthropic settings, while others are activists and organizers who are critical of mainstream, philanthropic approaches. Members also include those who have only ever been on the "asking" side of the funding equation, including those who have received SHIFT funding, and those who have been turned down for SHIFT funding. Furthermore, given that access to financial resources across society is deeply affected by systems of oppression related to race and gender (Block, Galabuzi, & Tranjan 2019), discussions at the Fund Disbursement Hub would be lacking in essential perspectives related to a diversity of systemic positionalities if racialized and gender-diverse members were absent.

Integrating the principle of meaningful diversity requires creating conditions that allow members to contribute — including the removal of financial barriers via an honorarium paid to all the participants in our decision-making structures who are not university employees.

> A big highlight for me is interacting with the other members — the diversity aspect of the members. Not just how we "look" — how we represent diversity; we come from different places and see our role in society differently. But there

is also a hidden diversity — other ways of knowing that are
hidden within ourselves. The diversity of those diverse ways of
knowing is also apparent in the steering committee members.
[…]. Having people from different ways of knowing coming
together, [and] also allowing those people to share.
(Ezgi Ozyonum, SHIFT SC member)

Meaningful diversity enriches discussion and results in more well-rounded
strategy decisions. Our commitment to gathering diverse perspectives
is anchored in SHIFT's mission, vision, values and ways of working that
ground all decision-making and make it possible to find ways forward,
even in conflictual situations.

Principle two: Think from the centre

We invite governance members to bring their whole selves to the table
when contributing to discussion as opposed to speaking as representatives
of any group. For instance, when establishing the criteria to select the types
of projects that would receive funding, members of the SC might expect the
other members who are climate activists to be trying to ensure that projects
with an environmental focus would have priority; that those from the social
entrepreneurship sector would be arguing for the importance of initiatives
working toward financial self-sufficiency; and that the arts-based social
change practitioners would want creativity to be at the centre. To address this
risk, we practice articulating the difference between being in a "representation" role and being asked to contribute to the group's collective reflection
on a question from a place of one's own experiences and perspectives.

Thinking from the centre draws a visual analogy of a round table of
committee members, where all concerns and ideas of any member have
been brought to the centre of the table for consideration. At the centre of
the table is also our grounding in the shared purpose that has assembled
the committee: a commitment to SHIFT's vision, mission and values. For
instance, an Ecosystem Activation hub member who is a Concordia student
may also be the only person in the group with a background in the pure
sciences, while also being the only first-generation university attendee. On
any subject of decision-making, any one of these aspects of their experience might contribute valuable insight. As the student has neither been
designated by the Concordia student body to represent their interests on
the committee nor has SHIFT asked them to be in the role of "student representative," they can bring their perspective informed by any aspect of their

experience, allowing us as "wholes" to relate to each other as collectivities (Riddle 2018). Making space for the complex and intersecting identities that inform members' perspectives on issues related to social transformation and systemic injustice contributes to decision-making informed by the richness of our community.

One way that we enact this principle is by how we frame proposals and strategic questions that are brought to governance committees. For instance, when asking for approval of our annual budget with the SC, we use framing such as, "Does this budget align with the strategic priorities that we collectively set last month?" as opposed to, "Do you approve this budget?" This framing supports governance members in bringing concerns or objections related to elements of shared decisions that have already been developed, instead of individual reflections that may be influenced by personal preference or experience. Similarly, after a long discussion where many issues have been raised about a proposal, we might encourage members to take a few minutes to pause and reflect on how they might see the proposal differently, considering all the needs and concerns that have been raised through the conversation. This encourages others to respond from a place of care for all the factors that have been raised, as opposed to their personal concerns.

Principle three: Normalizing dissent

Seeking consent in a context of meaningful diversity will occasionally lead to disagreement. That's the idea. This is not always comfortable, and it is rarely easy. The challenge of raising concerns can also be experienced as much more difficult for people with less structural power within the group. However, these perspectives are needed to ensure that the course of action will be adapted to the needs or interests of more marginalized groups. These considerations are of paramount importance in the field of social innovation and social change, where the primary objectives are to respond to social issues that disproportionately affect structurally disempowered communities. As one SC member contends:

> The framing of diversity really opens space for people to have different knowledges and disagree and it's normal. Because SHIFT exists within a learning facility, debate is seen as healthy and productive. It's more like — "if no one questions it, there must be something wrong." That's really different from the feeling in other spaces, where we feel like there is no time and

a decision has to be made right now. At SHIFT, in two hours, people can speak what they think, clearly, and make the decision. (Nafija Rahman, SHIFT SC member)

To counteract some of our conditioning around discomfort with dissent, we use a variety of approaches to create an organizational culture where "vibrant clashes" (Mouffe, 2000; 2013; 2017) and dissensus (Rancière, 2004; 2015) are seen as a natural and healthy part of any decision-making process around complex and nuanced questions such as those involved in social transformation. An important tool is to highlight the desire for the diversity of perspectives to bring to light new information that aids the development of shared decisions. There is a clear role for skillful facilitation, whereby dissent can be welcomed when it is spoken, while also creating space for others in the group to express their recognition or support for this dissenting opinion.

We also use a multi-step process for consent-based decision-making. This includes individual reflection, structured discussions and straw polls to ensure everyone's voice is heard (see Figure 13). This process includes time for individual reflection and discussion formats, such as rounds where each person is asked to speak in turn as opposed to relying predominantly on open discussion, which can be easily dominated by a select few voices (Karpowitz, Mendelberg, & Shaker, 2012). Planning for a meeting agenda to include these elements creates the conditions for meeting participants to experience coherence between the facilitator's statements that their dissent is valuable to the process, and their experience in voicing it.

The experience of being able to come to important and timely decisions within a diverse group is regularly cited by governance participants as one of the most valuable experiences that they have had with SHIFT. The experience of interacting as equals and engaging in generative dialogue with people coming from different positions of structural power and different approaches to engaging in social change has had a powerful effect on some of their self-perceptions and their sense of hope about the potential for change. Members repeatedly cite their incredulity that the group can start from places of dissent and divergence and, throughout a two-hour meeting, move toward a decision they can all stand behind. They also come to see how many other aspects of our lives could be far more effectively and compassionately organized.

The resources required to manage this type of governance system are not negligible. We estimate that between five to ten percent of our organizational resources are invested in staff time and honoraria required to administer, structure, and facilitate our model, and compensate the members involved. For many organizations, this type of investment can seem daunting, particularly if they are operating in a context where the pressures of donor priorities incentivize low overhead and administrative expenses. However, our mission is deeply enhanced by the accountability and engagement of our members throughout our decision-making processes. With social transformation at the heart of everything we do, the investment in dynamic, community-led governance is the surest way we know to create conditions that generate the ideas, experiments, evidence, and lasting systemic change that we are working toward.

CASE EXAMPLE: FIRSTHAND ACCOUNT OF SHIFT'S IMPACT

The following account written by Kristen Young illustrates the various pathways of engagement one person can have while working with SHIFT. Kristen has been a Governance Hub member since 2021; she also participated in two SHIFT-funded project teams and multiple juries, and she is now Secretary of the Board at the Black Healing Centre (BHC).

The BHC is a physical space of healing for Black people in Tio'tia:ke (Montreal). Through our work, we seek to counteract the trauma that comes with the Black experience and the poverty that is enacted by systemic racism. Through various free and subsidized therapy sessions and alternative, holistic wellness programs, BHC offers physical and virtual spaces for Black folks to connect and heal their traumas together. SHIFT's goals of facilitating connections and deep knowledge sharing between Concordians and external stakeholders provided an avenue through which BHC could connect and become a part of the SHIFT ecosystem.

Specifically, through the Gateway Funding program for teams committed to learning and working toward social change — through community-grounded projects tackling inequity, injustice and unsustainability — BHC was able to run "Healing Through Art Days." This program consisted of a monthly curated space of healing for Black people to help alleviate social isolation and symptoms of Seasonal Affective Disorder, by creating a communal space where people came and engaged in self- and communal healing. We were able to provide the facilitators with a living wage while keeping the program free for participants, which was essential for increasing participation in wellness activities for those who are often systemically barred from mental health and wellness.

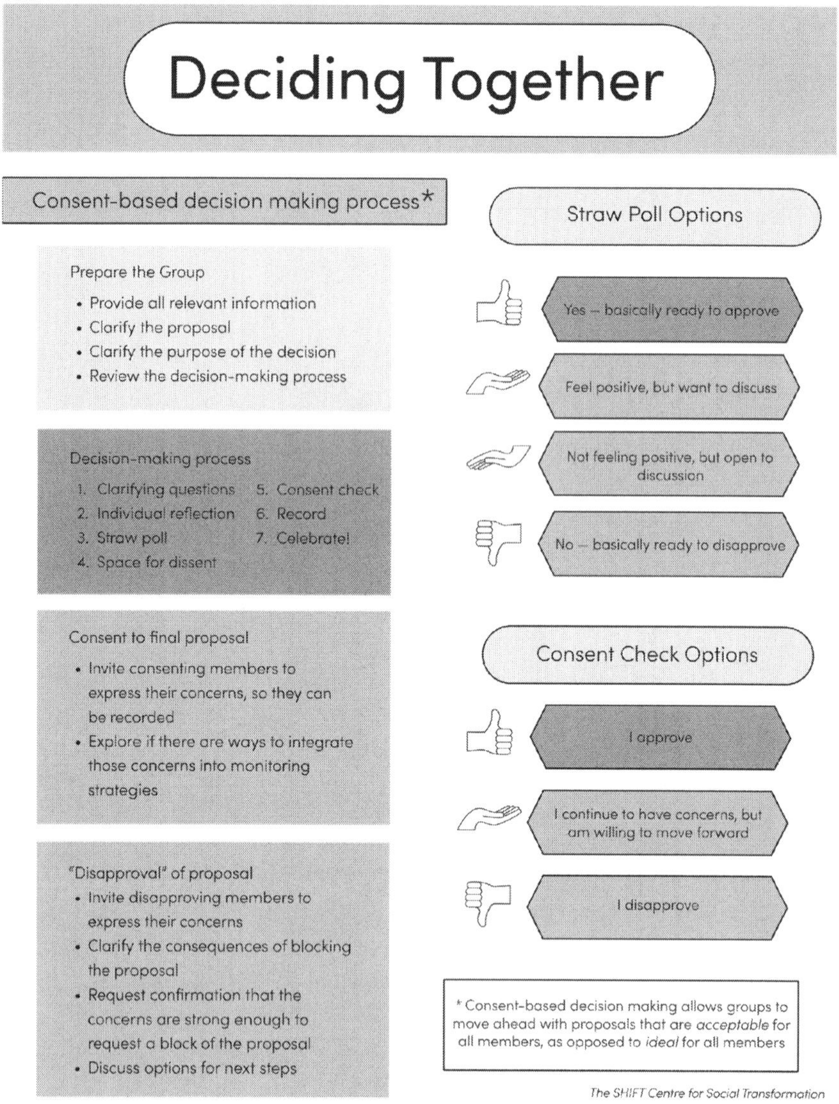

98 INTERRUPTING INNOVATION

Deciding Together

Consent-based decision making process*

Prepare the Group
- Provide all relevant information
- Clarify the proposal
- Clarify the purpose of the decision
- Review the decision-making process

Decision-making process
1. Clarifying questions
2. Individual reflection
3. Straw poll
4. Space for dissent
5. Consent check
6. Record
7. Celebrate!

Consent to final proposal
- Invite consenting members to express their concerns, so they can be recorded
- Explore if there are ways to integrate those concerns into monitoring strategies

"Disapproval" of proposal
- Invite disapproving members to express their concerns
- Clarify the consequences of blocking the proposal
- Request confirmation that the concerns are strong enough to request a block of the proposal
- Discuss options for next steps

Straw Poll Options

- Yes — basically ready to approve
- Feel positive, but want to discuss
- Not feeling positive, but open to discussion
- No — basically ready to disapprove

Consent Check Options

- I approve
- I continue to have concerns, but am willing to move forward
- I disapprove

* Consent-based decision making allows groups to move ahead with proposals that are *acceptable* for all members, as opposed to *ideal* for all members

The SHIFT Centre for Social Transformation

Figure 13: "Deciding Together," from the SHIFT Centre for Social Transformation.

Further, to make the in-person events welcoming, where folks can be themselves, open and vulnerable, we provided everything needed to participate (e.g., art materials, bus tickets, snacks). Active listeners were also present so that if the conversation were triggering to any participants, they were allowed to step away with someone whose role was to hear them and give them whatever support they needed at that moment. Our participants have taught us that validation and recognition are a great first step to creating safer spaces and opening the door to further wellness journeys. SHIFT's funding allowed us to not only provide programming to improve the mental health and wellness of our community but also allowed us to make our social justice ideals a reality. These funding practices mirrored the validation and recognition that we sought to build into our program. By ensuring the participants could attend barrier-free; by providing for them within the space; and by paying those making the program a reality appropriately, SHIFT demonstrated an understanding of how intertwined community well-being can be. The needs of those who do care work and of those who receive care must both be considered for a program like "Healing Through Art Days" to be successful.

BHC relationship with SHIFT could have easily ended with this initial funding. However, the Gateway Funding program was not meant to be transactional—it was a meeting place, not a tollbooth. Receiving funding made BHC a part of SHIFT's Learning Community, with an array of individuals and organizations who were each working toward social transformation in their own ways. This community allowed BHC to broaden its network of partners and collaborators to include organizations, such as the Refugee Centre, as well as various Concordia departments, such as the Black Perspectives Office. The connections we made helped develop ways of working and thinking, while also providing access to resources and a wider, socially innovative community than BHC would have had on its own.

Through a community connection, BHC is now part of a community-university research partnership called "Community Centered Knowledges: Fostering Black Wellness in Montreal." This project seeks to bring primarily Black thinkers, organizers and people with lived experience together to understand how we think, do and invent sustainable, race-aware, equitable, community-level responses to the wellness needs of Montreal's Black community. These conversations and understandings will then be reflected to the community through a virtual knowledge hub accessible to all. SHIFT is a gateway through which BHC can bring the community into the university and social innovation into an academic space.

SHIFT has also recently reinvested in BHC through the Deep Investment Fund, a funding program for project teams tackling significant community-identified issues related to inequity, injustice and unsustainability. BHC is working with Dr. Lisa Ndejuru and Concordia's Department of Applied Human Sciences to pilot a Community Care Practitioners Program, which will train Black practitioners to provide one-on-one wellness care, anchored in an Afro-positive approach to address this gap in the community. SHIFT's reinvestment allows BHC to demonstrate the legitimacy of its healing framework through the practices of the university. Moreover, BHC is exploring a collaboration with Concordia Continuing Education which would turn the pilot into a program to certify practitioners. This benefit straddles the boundary between the university and the community, and speaks to the ability of SHIFT and its ecosystem to transform the university from within.

Beyond the direct material benefit of funding, individuals and organizations within the SHIFT ecosystem may participate in relationship-building and foster connection, growth, and social innovation in a variety of ways. I have experienced several of these pathways to participation. Firstly, funding juries are spaces where we can truly see innovation and power sharing at work. My own experiences on juries were related to growing the SHIFT ecosystem and selecting individuals who would become part of the hubs and committees that govern SHIFT. The jury decided whom we would select, and given that dissent is encouraged, conversations were always lively and allowed us to come eventually to a shared decision.

Secondly, the SHIFT Governance Hub is tasked with keeping an eye on SHIFT's governance structure as a whole and ensuring its alignment with the mission. Tangibly, that looks like working with individuals at all levels of SHIFT to ensure they understand its multi-layered nature, where they fit within it, the power they hold within it, the communication avenues where their resources and supports are, etc. It has been inspiring to see the ways the community and the university have come together within and around SHIFT to understand the ways its internal governance is complex and ever-evolving, and to think about the ways SHIFT's very existence is altering Concordia's internal landscape.

Finally, as a funded-project team, the BHC can host student interns each semester. SHIFT coordinates with Concordia departments and arranges for students who are looking to spend their internship hours with a community organization and covers the cost of the student's wage. For BHC, this made participation in the internship program extremely beneficial as it fits well with our organization's values of paying especially racialized and marginalized folks for the labour they produce, regardless of the circumstances. Not surprisingly, internships become the pathway through which students are exposed to the socially transformative nature of the centre, and as a result, some students join the SHIFT ecosystem in a variety of ways.

This is one person's perspective of a handful of touchpoints around social innovation in SHIFT. There are so many others. From interns to project teams to staff to faculty, folks can come as they are; more so, they can bring all of who they are to bear in a manner that is self-reinforcing and drives social innovation rooted in shared humanity and sustainability, which comes from developing an ecosystem together in response to real needs in the community.

CONCLUSION

In this chapter, we proposed that in pursuing social innovation work, groups must consider not just what they plan to do, but how they plan to do it together. Social transformation is not a static exercise; thus, it is important to adopt an approach to managing this transformation that is responsive to the broader context. Dynamic systems of governance such as those discussed here are important tools for formalizing community leadership and accountability to stakeholders within social innovation spaces. Furthermore, these structures provide a basis for developing a culture of community ownership, community care and genuine valuation of diverse viewpoints. Finally, given that the deliberation that is central to seeking consent in diverse contexts can act as a catalyst for exploring alternatives, it may be a foundational element for initiating responsive social innovations that work for the communities they purport to serve. Power-sharing structures should be a feature of social innovation organizations for them to maintain their radical potential.

Further, in a context where complex problems call for dialogue and negotiation, the absence of deliberative organizations in the daily lives of average citizens restricts the scope and depth of our ability to work together on challenging problems (Felicetti, 2018). Cases like that of SHIFT demonstrate how we might build up the deliberative capacity of citizens in how we work together across and within organizations on pressing local issues, while engaging those who are affected by decisions. The case of SHIFT demonstrates what can come out of a purposeful engagement with a process of co-design that is not just of objectives and goals, but is an entire approach to working together. Democracy of any sort is a process that involves a continued redistribution of power and the purposeful development of dynamic systems of governance.

Reflection Questions

1. If you were to explain the notion of self-management and/or dynamic systems of governance to someone new to these concepts, how would you do it?
2. What connections do you see between systems of self-governance and broader social justice objectives?
3. What is the proposed relationship between models of self-governance and consent-seeking, decision-making in a case like SHIFT?
4. In what way might the process and structure of *how* we organize have an impact on *what* we organize to do?

ACKNOWLEDGEMENTS

As with every element of our work at SHIFT, this chapter — and the reflections and conversations that made it possible — were the fruit of collective efforts. In addition to the co-authors listed above, we would like to acknowledge the contributions of members across the SHIFT community, in particular: SHIFT staff members; steering committee members; and members of all of the SHIFT hubs. We wish to acknowledge also the powerful, socially transformative work carried out by the funded project teams.

REFERENCES

Bate, P., Khan, R., & Pye, A. (2000). Towards a culturally sensitive approach to organization structuring: Where organization design meets organization development. *Organization Science, 11*(2), 197–211.

Bjorgvinsson, E., Ehn, P., & Hillgren, P-A. (2012). Agonistic participatory design: Working with marginalised social movements. *CoDesign, 8* (2–3), 127–44.

Block, S., Galabuzi, G.E., & Tranjan, R. (2019). Canada's colour coded income inequality. *Canadian Centre for Policy Alternatives,* (December), 1–26.

Boeke, K. (1945). Sociocracy: Democracy as it might be. *Sociocracy: A Deeper Democracy.* www.sociocracy.info/sociocracy-democracy-kees-boeke/

Brand, T. (2020). Stakeholder dialogue as agonistic deliberation: Exploring the role of conflict and self-interest. *Business Ethics Quarterly, 30*(1), 3–30.

Buck, J., & Villines, S. (2007). *We the people: Consenting to a deeper democracy.* (2nd ed). Sociocracy Info Press.

Christensen, C.M., Raynor, M.E., & McDonald, R. (2015). What is disruptive innovation? *Harvard Business Review, 93*(12), 44–53.

Daft, R.L., Murphy, J., & Willmott, H. (2020). *Organization theory & design: An international perspective* (4th ed.). Cengage.

Denis, J-L., Lamothe, L., & Langley, A. (2001). The dynamics of collective leadership and strategic change in pluralistic organizations. *Academy of Management Journal, 44*(4), 809–837.

Diefenbach, T. 2019. Why Michels' "iron law of oligarchy" is not an iron law — and how democratic organisations can stay "oligarchy-free." *Organization Studies, 40*(4), 545–562.

Ehrenfeld, J.R. (2009). *Sustainability by design: A subversive strategy for transforming our consumer culture.* Yale University Press.

Ercan, S.A., & Dryzek, J.S. (2015). The reach of deliberative democracy. *Policy Studies, 36*(3), 241–248.

Escobar, A. (2018). *Designs for the pluriverse: Radical interdependence, autonomy, and the making of worlds.* Duke University Press.

Felicetti, A. (2018). A deliberative case for democracy in firms. *Journal of Business Ethics, 150*(3), 803–814.

Follett, M. P. (1925). Constructive conflict. In Bureau of Personnel Administration Conference.

Gladu, C., Paquin, R.L., & Prakash, R. (2020). The good fight: Constructive conflict by design. *Academy of Management Proceedings, 2020* (1), 15121.

Isaacs, W. (1999). *Dialogue and the art of thinking together: A pioneering approach to communicating in business and in life.* Crown Business.

Isaacs, W. (2001). Toward an action theory of dialogue. *International Journal of Public Administration, 24*(7/8), 709–748.

Kania, J., Kramer, M., & Senge, P. (2018, June). *The water of systems change.* FSG. www.fsg.org/resource/water_of_systems_change/#resource-downloads.

Karpowitz, C.F., Mendelberg, T., & Shaker, L. (2012). Gender inequality in deliberative participation. *American Political Science Review, 106*(3), 533–547.

Klein, N. (2015). *This changes everything: Capitalism vs. the climate.* Simon and Schuster.

Lee, M.Y., & Edmondson, A.C. (2017). Self-managing organizations: Exploring the limits of less-hierarchical organizing. *Research in Organizational Behavior, 37,* 35–58.

Lefebvre, H. (1976). *The survival of capitalism: Reproduction of the relations of production.* St. Martin's Press.

Manz, C.C., Shipper, F.M., & Stewart, G.L. (2009). Everyone a team leader: Shared influence at W. L. Gore & Associates. *Organizational Dynamics, 38*(3), 239–244.

Martin, R.L., & Osberg, S. (2007). Social entrepreneurship: The case for definition. *Stanford Social Innovation Review, 5*(2), 28–39.

Mouffe, C. (1999). Deliberative democracy or agonistic pluralism? *Social Research, 66*(3), 745–759.

Mouffe, C. (2000). Deliberative democracy or agonistic pluralism. *Reihe Politikwissenschaft - Political Science Series, 72.*

Mouffe, C. (2013). *Agonistics: Thinking the world politically.* Verso Books.

Mouffe, C. (2017). Rewriting democracy. Routledge.

Ospina, S.M., & Saz-Carranza, A. (2010). Paradox and collaboration in network management. *Administration & Society, 42*(4), 404–440.

Ostrom, E. (1990). *Governing the commons.* Cambridge University Press.

Raelin, J.A. (2014). Imagine there are no leaders: Reframing leadership as collaborative agency. *Leadership, 12*(2), 131–158.

Rancière, J. (2004). Introducing disagreement. *Angelaki: Journal of the Theoretical Humanities 9*(3), 3–9.

Rancière, J. (2015). *Dissensus: On politics and aesthetics.* Bloomsbury Publishing.

Riddle, E. (2018, December 10). (Indigenous) governance is gay. *GUTS.* www.gutsmagazine.ca/indigenous-governance-is-gay/.

Romme, A., & Georges, L. (2003). Making a difference: Organization as design. *Organization Science, 14*(5), 558–573.

Romme, A., & Georges, L. (2004). Unanimity rule and organizational decision making: A simulation model. *Organization Science, 15*(6), 704–718.

104 INTERRUPTING INNOVATION

Romme, A., Georges, L., Broekgaarden, J., Huijzer, C., Reijmer, A. &, van der Eyden, R.A.I. (2016). From competition and collusion to consent-based collaboration: A case study of local democracy. *International Journal of Public Administration, 41*(3), 246–255.

Romme, A., Georges, L., & Endenburg, G. (2006). Construction principles and design rules in the case of circular design. *Organization Science, 17*(2), 287–297.

Romme, A., Georges L., & Van Witteloostuijn, A. (1999). Circular organizing and triple loop learning. *Journal of Organizational Change Management, 12*(5), 439–453.

Semler, R. (1989). Managing without managers. *Harvard Business Review, 67*(5), 76–84.

SHIFT. (n.d.). Governance Recruitment. Concordia University. www.concordia.ca/content/concordia/en/about/shift/vision/governance/recruitment.html

Shipper, F., Manz, C.C., & Stewart, G.L. (2014). W. L. Gore & Associates: Developing global teams to meet twenty-first-century challenges. In S.B. Adams (Ed.), *Shared entrepreneurship: A path to engaged employee ownership* (pp. 267–284). Springer.

Taibbi, M. (2014). *The divide: American injustice in the age of the wealth gap.* Spiegel & Grau.

Tsoukas, H. (2009). A dialogical approach to the creation of new knowledge in organizations. *Organization Science, 20*(6), 941–957.

Life Imitates Art

Collage as Innovative Pedagogy

Ken Moffatt and Reena Tandon

> **Learning Objectives**
>
> 1. Think about how arts-based pedagogy helps students and professors to reflect critically on their agency for social justice and social change through image and text.
> 2. Consider collage as a pedagogical tool, as well as an arts-based process and outcome.
> 3. Rethink resistance to social change contrary to online commercial technologies and other taken-for-granted social texts and roles.

COLLAGE, WHICH IS OFTEN THOUGHT OF as the regrouping of images (most often pre-existing) into a single work, brings into question the original image; produces a tension between images; and, at its most exhilarating, creates new meaning altogether. Collage helps us to imagine a new world by questioning taken-for-granted social relations and thought (Gurney & Haladyn, 2022). Collage acts as social innovation in pedagogy in that it helps students imagine new social possibilities and engages students and professors in the practice of social justice communication by creating, through text and image, new forms of communication. As educators, we take up collage as an art form, as a medium for activism and advocacy, and as a means to express personal and social concepts. As with the examples of arts-based interventions discussed in Chapter 3, our work with the artistic medium of collage becomes a form of meaning-making that engages us as participants in imagining a socially transformed society and provides a space to pause, reflect and allow fragments "to be."

Collage provides a connection to academic learning and to lived experience. In addition, as Gurney and Haladyn (2022) state, collage is never singular; rather, it builds communities. This opportunity is valuable for students to connect with the larger social issues, as well as with their peers who share similar passions. Collage projects work against the empty aggregation of research for text and images by asking for an analysis and a reconfiguration of text and images. This work has wide-ranging educational benefits for the students as they become conscious of text/image and of the modes of digital research, and learn how to reconstruct collage so that they can put their own touch on the material.

We discuss our journey related to introducing collage as a pedagogy to classrooms and community settings. We argue that collage is a form of education, as well as an art form, that engages students in innovative modes of learning. At the same time, our pedagogical approach during this particular time took on an innovative, reflexive form akin to the qualities of collage, as the unexpected kept introducing itself into the project's development. Collage came to the fore, both inadvertently and intentionally, as a means to make sense of teaching and learning through moments that were not easily defined due to changing social contexts.

We thus report on a project that is innovative in that it: spans disciplinary affinity; puts into play inclusive, creative pedagogy and learning; and engages students in participatory learning. Central to the project is the multi-year relationship between the authors, based in discussion and reflection on education. This project came into play when both of us held university leadership roles that offered transdisciplinary learning opportunities across our urban campus. Our cross-faculty positions had a tremendous reach, serving thousands of students across dozens of programs. Reena was (and still is) chair of **Community Engaged Learning and Teaching** (CELT) in the Faculty of Arts; and Ken was the Jack Layton Chair in the Faculty of Arts and Faculty of Community Services, and he continues as a professor of social work at Toronto Metropolitan University (TMU).

Our inclusion of collage in teaching sociology, criminology and social work courses included introducing an exercise open to multiple ways of learning. An additional goal of our pedagogy was to support students to question the nature of knowledge, including its delivery online. Specific objectives of our pedagogy were related to course-based content, such as the expansion and diversification of the canon of sociology by highlighting individuals and ideas neglected by Western, heteronormative founders of classical social theory. In criminology, news items were integrated into collage to combine theoretical concepts with the social practices of criminology. Social work course objectives included: thinking through how the personal and political are interconnected for practice; exploring art as a socially transformative practice; examining the representation of marginalized communities; and researching resistance to social change. Collage helped rethink imagery while dealing with radical inclusiveness in education so that we and the students patched together a "crazy quilt," or in other words, a collage.

THEORETICAL UNDERPINNINGS

According to Judith Butler (2006a, 2006b), images and text are discourse whereby what is uttered is integrated with the exercise of power. Butler mostly focused on gender to elaborate the concept of discourse that can be used across a wide variety of social conditions and social identities. Key to understanding discourse is that there is no essential meaning beyond the uttering of a word or showing of images. Often, discourse operates without transparency of its social and political purpose but is assumed as social practices that are taken for granted. The idea that power exists at the point of utterance is revelatory for a contemporary classroom comprised of students who are engaged in both online and in-person realities, and who, in their private lives, are constantly negotiating a sea of imagery (Kristeva, 2002; Moffatt, 2019). The power of discourse (including image and text) is manifested through its repetition. Through constant repetition, discourses about race, gender and sexuality take on a taken-for-granted quality that defines social possibilities. This repetition is not the sole expression of individual subjects but rather involves social patterns that both enable and constrain a subject (Butler, 1993).

French sociologist Pierre Bourdieu (1988) struggled with the conflict that existed between the objectivist and subjectivist approaches to sociology. He argued that too often the objectivist approach became the dominant one to human affairs. This struggle continues through academia today with reductionist, technocratic and scientistic approaches to knowledge and research being most highly valued (Moffatt, 2019). Bourdieu works around this conflict using the concept of **participant objectivation**. This approach involves those who are observers being fully engaged in the exercise at the point of observation rather than standing apart. We turn our instruments of observation and analysis back on ourselves. The students can, with this approach, engage in a type of reflexive practice whereby they consider the taken-for-grantedness of discourse on the internet; their own relationship to language and images; and their subjective, reflexive engagement in this network of discourses (Tandon, Moffatt, & Furmli, 2021).

During an interview, South African artist William Kentridge (2023), a collage artist and an advocate of the politics of collage, points out that it is important to understand that both optimistic and pessimistic futures are unrolling at once. It is best to acknowledge these disruptions in the political world where things shift and change. According to Kentridge, collage as a mode of art practice, social practice and way of thinking is important for keeping us open to and aware of important political practices. Collage can also work as a mode of resistance, as will be illustrated in the examples provided below using the collage work of students and community members. The collages are about different historical and contemporary moments, based at times on social movements; at other times, they address and capture more elusive concerns for change.

Kentridge (2023) talks of the vital importance of working against dominant narratives (such as the universalizing discourse of the professional; or the reductionist and scientific approaches to political and social affairs) to advocate for a type of **provisional coherence**. Provisional coherence allows for narratives that include emotion, ambiguity, contradiction — even absurdity. That is, the coherence that takes the many elements of a life, of a narrative, and combines them so that lives and history are reconstructed from fragments. In this manner, as we recombine life as a form of collage, we are also active in reconstructing the world.

Robert O'Meally (2022) discusses the importance of collage to African American communities in the US. Like Kentridge, he argues for the importance of patching together practices, language and images to work against domination — in this case, against racism. O'Meally argues that collage is much more than putting together fragments to create an identity; the act of collage enriches and deepens identity for African Americans. In the examples discussed below, we draw on the concept of **antagonistic cooperation** whereby the wide diversity of cultural expression and thought is valued in the development of art.

According to O'Meally (2022), we not only learn to listen to the most dissonant voice or thought but we also learn to value them through our own improvisation. To use the metaphor of jazz, we respect and hear the other's voice while moving beyond tolerance of diversity. The expression by each of us may be marked by antagonism but we eventually enrich our own voices/creations by hearing new harmonies that once sounded like noise. Rather than strive for a perfect accord, we live with the push and pull of each other to make new ideas and art that can sustain all of us. The intent is to move together, while acknowledging differences, to the point that we work together for transcendent goals through the practice of patching together disparate voices, ideas and texts. Key to conscientious discussion is to include all those who have been left out of the discussion or left behind socially.

COLLAGE

Often described as emerging in 1912, as the creation of Georges Braque and Pablo Picasso, collage has been typically defined as the use of papers, including manufactured images, with glue-based adhesive (Blake, 2023; Vaughan, 2005). In fact, collage has a much wider socio-cultural context, as well as a more complex history. A form of collage, for example, can be linked to *Tsugigami,* an artistic practice that dates back to the twelfth century in Japan (Blake, 2023). Based on this more complicated historical understanding of collage, the term has a wide variety of definitions, often based on the artist's method as well as intent for the practice (Blake, 2023; Gurney & Haladyn, 2022; Vaughan, 2005). In a contemporary context, collage has expanded greatly to include work that is exhibited in pop-up shows and studio visits, and posted on social media and the internet. The documentation of the many forms of collage can be elusive and its legacy can be fleeting (Blake, 2023).

At the beginning of this project, collage was mostly conceptualized by the authors as analog collage. Analog collage involves elements of collage that are hand-cut and then mechanically pieced together by hand. However, through the many iterations of the project and in light of the complex context of our educational institution (that involves participants who are diverse according to race, age, gender, sexuality, ability and class), our definition of collage has expanded over time. The scope of collage associated with the project now includes the following: *anticollage,* a process whereby the artist re-touches or removes elements of an existing image or picture either by putting treatment over elements of the image, removing parts of the image or crossing out elements while leaving them visible; *bricolage,* another process that became an important part of the project (particularly since some phases of the project involved participation during a pandemic lockdown), includes whatever elements or objects are part of the maker's life and near-at-hand, or in the possession of the artist, including items such as receipts or jewelry, and so on, rather than items that are sourced or researched; *digital collage,* which involves creating a collage that is made in part or entirely by electronic means; and *found collage,* a form of orchestrated chance, is made from material found while walking, including materials that may or may not be considered detritus (Blake, 2023).

In the city of Toronto, a vital art movement developed, focused on appropriation. This movement offers a good starting point for understanding collage for the purposes of this chapter. Appropriation involves bringing disparate images together so that new meaning is created. The collage form of appropriation involves the relocation of an image from one context to another to create various effects, including creating new meanings from the montage of fragments; a reinterpretation of common and taken-for-granted visual culture; and a way of interpreting the world to disrupt a stationary viewpoint (Gurney & Haladyn, 2022). New meaning can happen through the collision or coherence of images that are often from different time periods, people or places.

For Toronto-based Indigenous artist Carl Beam, collage reimagines history and time as nonlinear rather than the mainstream's approach to history, which is linear and progressive. According to Beam, nonlinear time is more in keeping with Indigenous ways of knowing so that meaning is "moving all over the place" (cited in Jordan-Haladyn, 2022, p. 96). Collage offers a way of thinking about, feeling and imagining a world without constraint. For Beam, collage is a means to wipe away history, to experience dream time in your mind. It offers a means to correct linear, written history by raising the centrality of the event through collage. Because collage is nonlinear with no single point of view, it is open to polyphonic qualities (Jordan-Haladyn, 2022).

Writing about Norwegian-Nigerian artist Frida Orupabo's representation of time through her collage work, Portia Malatjie (2023) comments on the continued social experience of Black South Africans, describing a type of "extreme waiting," whether for basic services, infrastructure or fundamental human rights. The waiting is "in effect, waiting *to matter*," "a pain reserved for those forced to operate from the periphery" (original emphasis). She comments on the ongoing persecution and prejudicial treatment of Black people twenty-eight years after the dissolution of apartheid. Malatjie goes on to note how, through the exclusive use of found imagery, Orupabo started collage based on her own visual archive. Trained as a sociologist and having worked before that at a resource centre for sex workers and those who had been trafficked, Orupabo's collages centre Black archival practice and the perpetual construction and deconstruction of the archive. Her work, argues Malatjie, invites "disquietude" through "discombobulated assemblages" that invite us to search for meaning and coherence in the image. Orupabo does not aspire to coherence, but rather, through pasting, cutting, braiding, splicing and weaving, she creates an intentional distortion of image (Malatjie, 2023).

INNOVATIVE TEACHING AND LEARNING THROUGH THE COLLAGE PROJECT

Our collage project originated in February 2020, with an invitation from gay male artist, author, critic, educator and writer-in-residence R.M. Vaughan (1965–2020) to Ken who asked him to participate in an online art project followed by an in-person gallery show in Fredericton at the University of New Brunswick. It was titled *Cut/Paste/Resist* (see @cut_paste_resist on Instagram). Reena was invited to be a third curator as we moved the project and the physical art exhibit to TMU. The plan was to have the exhibit travel to TMU since several entries were from our students; as well, the collage exhibit was well-matched to the university's goals of inclusion, diversity and community engagement. We planned to show collage in the TMU student centre and to provide workshops on collage at the exhibit. However, the plan of the project was disrupted by the arrival of COVID-19 in March 2020, which resulted in a lockdown of the university. The gallery show in the student centre was not possible at TMU nor was it possible to sponsor R.M. Vaughan to travel to the university for workshops and curation. We had to patch together a new plan from disparate pieces.

Reena had extended the project to student participation in the Faculty of Arts by adding a participatory element to humanities-based courses, starting with "Introduction to Sociology." In February 2020, we had also introduced the collage project to the Jack Layton Leadership School, leading a transdisciplinary, intensive, student-focused workshop across the Faculty of Arts and the Faculty of Community Services that focused on community leadership and participatory education. Shortly thereafter, we introduced collage as an assignment in two social work courses: "Power, Resistance and Change" and "Arts and Social Transformation."

Originally, the collage assignment was thought of as an educational opportunity based on the concept of direct action in a shared social environment with the enrichment of online exposure through Instagram (see @create_resist on Instagram). We chose the mode of antagonistic cooperation as a pedagogical process guiding the collage project, coupled with provisional coherence, to value our own ideas of equitable innovative learning and to be true to the nature of collage. The type of complex, social change of contemporary life on campus demanded a form of innovative education that could engage voices from the margins. Indeed, the project was originally envisioned to include in-person working sessions that would bring together students in collage-making workshops and discussions on campus. That action was to lead to further discussion about disparate ideas tied to student experience, especially the experience of marginalization. The intention was to build a progressive, social, change-oriented, multidisciplinary community across campus that would culminate in a large, public exhibit for civic engagement.

Of course, the exercise had to change direction due to COVID-19's arrival when all TMU classes were moved to an online format. As face-to-face educational opportunities collapsed, students were forced to remote learning. As educators, our plans had to be reshaped due to unforeseen circumstances. Our own reflexive pedagogical practice (Moffatt, 2019; Tandon, Moffatt & Furmli, 2021) and provisional coherence allowed us to rethink the project.

The delivery of the program was further complicated by the suicide of R.M. Vaughan (1965–2020), in October of 2020. The additional new challenge was how to remain true to our shared vision of social democracy and craft while taking a pause for our own grief. In short, this was a tremendous personal loss that created a pedagogical dilemma. This death occurred while students were already engaged in the collage project. In fact, the plan had been to have R.M. Vaughan attend TMU to hold workshops, to help curate an art exhibit and to be a guest lecturer in selected classrooms. After consultation among ourselves and with course directors, we decided to transform *Cut/Paste/Resist* into a new project focused on student work, entitled *Create Resist*.

At the same time, the collage assignment took on an enriched meaning in the context of virtual learning. Through the fall of 2020, classes were offered only remotely, online, due to the ongoing pandemic, and continued to be remote through all of 2021. Classes were hybrid at the start of 2022 and became in-person in the fall of 2022. We recalibrated the model and asked students to develop collages from any material available in their environment and/or those available digitally. This presented a unique opportunity for students to participate in, and learn about, online advocacy and public engagement through collage, as an accessible art form informed by theoretical understanding.

In the end, our feelings about the collage assignment as part of online teaching and learning moved from reluctance, to making readjustments to our original plan, to seeing the new direction as a tremendous success. It was an opportunity for creative engagement with students. The collage added vitality, social democracy and colour to online learning. The collage, and the presentations and discussions associated with the artwork, enlivened an online course shell and Zoom rooms with identity and social commentary, drawing both on image and text. Instructors found it a meaningful, activity-based learning opportunity that, in some ways, countered the problems with the compulsory, online teaching environment. Furthermore, students became engaged in thinking about and discussing how the online environment was affecting their epistemological and practice opportunities.

The process of adaptation and iteration of the CELT collage assignment deepened the meaning of collage. It broke the isolation of the students/young persons who created the collage. The assignment proved to be an innovative, pedagogical approach that provided a way to connect with the current social issues, as well as to take up an agential opportunity to think, express/create and participate (Bourdieu, 1989; Kentridge, 2022; O'Meally, 2022). It also was a means to further elaborate identity and think about other students' complex, differing identities.

Furthermore, because course-based learning was expanded to include the ability to create a collage from everyday materials available in the environment or from online images, learning and creating became accessible to all students. The students started to co-create shared meaning by creating a new presence in the learning environment in the presence of each other's differences. As Simmons and Daley (2013) found in their research, creating collage supports creators in making their tacit knowledge explicit, in reflecting at meta-cognitive levels and in transforming their thinking. For example, Jordan Danner, a sociology student, chose to address the taken-for-granted discursive structures of gender, sexuality and race by disrupting or queering "normal" patterns of expression.

Figure 14: *Untitled,* by Jordan Danner, from "Introduction to Sociology," Department of Sociology, TMU, 2021.

Students were also able to engage in the social and political issues close to campus in a manner that was nonlinear and could engage both local and international perspectives. Jeffery Simpson, a social work student, created a collage about the "War on Drugs," with an international component, yet still being very specific and local given that there had been a controversy on campus concerning a harm reduction clinic nearby. The presence of drug users on the streets near the campus had led to a discussion about social inclusion and exclusion so close to us.

In a theory course in sociology, students were invited to rethink theory through text and image based on the activism and thought of those who had been marginalized or silenced. For example, a group of students chose to focus on the thought and practice of suffragette Kate Sheppard.

Based on the success of the project in the online classroom environment, we continued to expand its reach to other courses in sociology, criminology and social work. Hundreds of students engaged in the project and some of the students decided to make their ideas public by voluntarily participating in *Create Resist* online (see Instagram profile @create_resist).

Figure 15: *Decriminalize*, by Jeffrey Simpson, from "Power, Resistance and Change," School of Social Work, TMU, 2022.

Figure 16: *Kate Sheppard*, by Keliah Cladwin, Kylie French, Jacques Lapointe and Alexandra Whelan, from "Classical Sociological Theory," Department of Sociology, 2022.

And still, the project evolved. In October 2022, we were part of a team of researchers who received a grant to explore the link between the crafts of art, research and pedagogy. We took the opportunity to develop the "Crafting Community Symposium," an in-person workshop for faculty members, students and community artists. It was also a means to reimagine community engagement as the safety regulations due to COVID-19 were in the process of being lifted.

The workshop took on similar principles to the original intent of the *Cut/Paste/Resist* project: it was structured to include community members, faculty and students in a participatory workshop. It was meant to be open and democratic so both professional and amateur artists could work side by side. The workshop was transdisciplinary in nature and was to engage participants directly in craft. We held an in-person workshop with restricted attendance for ten people in collaboration with author, poet, collage artist Camilla Gibb as a co-educator. The structure of the workshop included a neighbourhood stroll, where participants collected resources often thought of as detritus from the street and the lampposts to make collage on campus. We embraced collage, created from what was available locally, as a means to think about the public space around the university. Master of Social Work student Ada So took on the radical possibility of collage by combining found materials, including leaves, text and barcodes, with her own illustration. The barcodes captured the imagination of participants since we wondered what third-dimensional collage would be created when they were scanned and read.

Figure 17: *Connections,* by Ada So, from "Crafting Community Symposium," TMU, 2022.

Figure 18: From left to right, collages by Sandy McLeod, Jim Nason and Camilla Gibb, from "Crafting Community Symposium," on display at Bar Bacan in Toronto, 2022.

Upon presentation of the collages to each other, the participants discussed the nature of public space, the nature of campus space and the nature of online space, and, in each case, they intertwined the analysis with personal narrative. We were in-person again and thus able to introduce the possibility of building creative and progressive communities through the mode of collage. The collages created in the workshop were then shown publicly in a local restaurant. (For more information on the "Crafting Community Symposium," see "Workshop 2" at torontomu.ca/crafting-community-project/symposium/workshops/workshop_2/; and to see the ongoing research, please visit: torontomu.ca/crafting-community-project/ongoing_community_research/.)

COLLAGE AS INNOVATIVE PEDAGOGY

In addition to the special qualities of collage described above, we summarize two innovative, pedagogical qualities of the collage project that we iteratively learned while moving through changes in the project over time and changing circumstances. The collage assignment provided opportunities for students to engage with the concepts in their courses and translate them into visual representations. It also engaged them in imagining an audience or a collective for their work. With the potential for a wider audience, the students imagined how to communicate the focus on resistance, a theme across disciplines. In this section, we argue that, through collage, students moved from passive learning in the logocentric model to co-creation of meaning. Secondly, we note that collage offered an innovative way for students to think about the frames of their thought and creation.

Differing ways of knowing: Against logocentric thinking

Kentridge (2023) argues that working against logocentric thinking is a reason to become an artist. Logocentric thinking is driven by the cold logic of rational fact as if it is the only rigorous approach to truth (Moffatt, 2019). There is a rigour to collage, but this need not be tied to a fidelity to facts (Kentridge, 2023; Moffatt, 2019). Collage, with its intent to provoke the reader and viewer, is a challenge to the limits of how we teach and learn (Gurney & Haladyn, 2022; Vaughan, 2005). Collage can challenge the creator and the viewer politically, emotionally and conceptually. The collage project not only expands concepts that we work with in education, but also encourages students to create new scripts and texts. Students are encouraged to consider new ways of looking at the world not only as creators and co-creators, but also as witnesses to each other's work (Tandon, Moffatt, & Furmli, 2022).

By constructing assignments as a form of art, especially in conceptual classes such as sociology or criminology, one engages students in both action and knowledge creation. As Kentridge states, with art the expectation is that you invent the world. The world is there as raw material to be picked over by the artist or scavenged to invent images. For example, Emma Abramowitz,

Figure 19: *Untitled*, by Emma Abramowitz, from "Art and Social Transformation," School of Social Work, TMU, 2021.

a social work student, questions received social expectations and norms as they apply to gender through her elegant collage. She draws on found text, photography and her own illustration to take up the theme of resistance that challenges the authoritarian voice.

In talking about his own art practice, Kentridge (2023) articulates important principles that have been taken up by our collage project. Kentridge says that when working in the studio, one becomes acutely aware of fragmentation. Through the collage exercise, the students are encouraged to look for fragments, for meaning in fragments and for meaning between fragments (Tandon, Moffatt, & Furmli, 2020). According to Kentridge (2023), since the fragments exist in art creation, one becomes keenly aware that there is not one singular history or way of knowing, but a multitude of possible narrations of different events.

For our co-curator R.M. Vaughan, the importance of collage was the break from the bureaucratic and the obtuse, as well as from disconnected imagery that has no clear referent to craft or lived experience. In this manner, collage has an important political place in artistic expression since it is open to the unfinished, the slightly blemished and the eccentric (Moffatt, 2021a; Moffatt, 2021b; Vaughan cited in Burgos, 2020).

Working at the edge of the epistemological frame

According to Kentridge (2023), collage helps us think about how we construct coherence out of fragments. According to O'Meally (2022), we create a coherence that includes the most disparate elements and the most marginalized voices. When one takes something from the world, tears it into fragments and rearranges the fragments, those fragments become collage. This process involves an act of introspection and observation by others to imagine it as a construction that is coherent for others. It also reminds the student as a collage artist that we do not receive knowledge of the world, but construct it as we go through it (Kentridge, 2023; O'Meally, 2022).

The practice of collage helps one think about the frame within which we receive images, text and knowledge. What is essential about collage is not a "smooth narrative" that hides a troubled narrative of history and politics as lamented by Kentridge. Collage has rough edges and can be messy (Vaughan cited in Burgos, 2020). We become aware of the way the images are cut, placed together and piled up. As Etgar (2022, p. 48) states: collage involves a "preoccupation with the margins, edges or gaps that stop us from interpreting the picture as a carrier of information and enable us to see with fresh eyes." Collage offers the epistemological advantage of being a contested term. It has been disrupting expectations that things can be fully developed to be whole and perfect in one piece (Etgar, 2023). Collage is technical, due to materials and tools. It is a strategy based on conceptual principles; a historical object that belongs to specific technological eras; and a process. The frame is both the knowledge claim but also the mode of delivery (Moffatt, 2019; Moffatt, 2021b), including the internet, social media and commercial technologies.

As a commentary about the ongoing colonial representation of Black women, the artist Orupabo chose publicly available images from sources such as Instagram, eBay and Pinterest, but also archives from places like Getty and Alamy (Malatjie, 2023). To unshackle the visual identity of marginalized and Black people, she, at times, leaves companies' watermarks on images to display the repossession from capitalist visual monopolies — a reclamation of freedom. Hebony Haughten, a sociology student, takes a similar approach to reconstructing an epistemology of Black people by juxtaposing diverse, received, taken-for-granted imagery for our reconsideration.

120 INTERRUPTING INNOVATION

Figure 20: *How They See Us*, by Hebony Haughten, "Introduction to Sociology," Department of Sociology, TMU, 2021.

We also welcome collage as resistance to sterile, online imagery (Moffatt, 2019; Moffatt, 2021a). Any image that promises perfection or a "pure" form, particularly of gender, is suspect for its lack of complexity (Kristeva, 2002). R.M. Vaughan despised all art forms that were rendered so "pure" that they were lifeless and listless. In fact, perfection that created exclusion or shame was considered to be harmful (Moffatt, forthcoming; Moffatt, 2021b). Through the art form of collage, the voice of the artist can be faltering, the images can be referential and the artwork can look rough (Moffatt, 2021b). Despite the do-it-yourself quality, collage creates a new epistemology or way of thinking (Moffatt, 2019).

Working at the edge of the technological frame

With the wide reach of the internet and the ability to congregate images and text readily, Bishop (2023) argues that research has been replaced by the "search." Search-driven, arts-based research involves adhering to the search through pre-existing concepts that have been offered up by a search engine. In the post-digital age, thinking and research are not so much about making content, but rather about searching for content, configuring it and making meaning from it. Rather than take on their own research, artists download and assemble ideas and recontextualize material in a contemporary form of appropriation.

All our educational, technological platforms — Google Mail, Google Meets, D2L, Zoom, Facebook, Instagram — are commercial, money-making

Figure 21: *happy juice,* by Charlotte Fry, "Power, Resistance and Change," School of Social Work, TMU, 2021.

Figure 22: *Dear Google,* by Jennifer Li, "Art and Social Transformation," School of Social Work, TMU, 2021.

enterprises. These platforms tend to sanitize images for profit. For instance, anything that questions the profit-making centralization of power in the hands of a few is often made invisible on these platforms. Also, overtly political images that seek change in our socio-economic sphere are hidden or commercialized. As such, because such platforms have become compulsory for learning, students more than ever need to consider the frame. Charlotte Fry, a social work student/artist, took on the commercial aspects of received wisdom of women with her collage, but she also challenged modes of delivery through the commercialization of online platforms that contribute to gendered discourse.

Beyond making apparent the frame of technology by inviting students to use the class exercise for agency and meaning-making, their collage artwork enabled new, profound possibilities to come to the fore. The students actively subverted impersonal technologies of education, at times, by personalizing their messages; imagining new social possibilities and futures; or engaging in social messages beyond the fractured, socio-economic reality of the moment. For example, Jennifer Li, a social work student and advocate for persons experiencing eating disorders, used collage as a form of resistance against the very platforms we were using.

CONCLUSION

In this chapter, we argue for the importance of moving beyond the logo-centric approach to education to a more engaged and aesthetic approach. We also argue for the importance of students working at the edge of taken-for-granted epistemological structures and knowledge claims. This invites a form of engaged pedagogy whereby the student is present and challenges the limits of knowledge claims, as well as the structure of online platforms and their assumptions.

The ability to rethink method and purpose is at the heart of social innovation. Collage allowed students to comment on, discuss and even feel part of the social movements. Through collage, they talked about social fragmentation and put forth their own analytic, felt, idiosyncratic touch. We hope collage also helped them to enrich their sense of identity through their attainment of a multi-layered understanding of how elements fit together.

Throughout the pedagogical journey outlined above, collage became much more than a tool for learning. In our quest to find ways to reach students and instructors, and to find a pause for reflection, collage was appealing for its simple, uncomplicated, open-ended nature. Collage provided a language for students so that they were able to combine the self, the text and the context. It also influenced us as educators.

Without the elaborate structure of live, in-person events imagined in the first iteration of *Cut/Paste/Resist,* we were still able to help students imagine communities and form connections through the project *Create Resist.* The collages provided us with windows into the ways that students are assimilating the text and the world, both through their shared personal experiences as well as their ongoing questions. Collage provided a way for us to face our own angst over the pedagogical, social and economic context, and to marvel at futures possible through the felt experience and emotional commitments of the students. We learned from them and each other as we paused, reconsidered and pieced together an approach open to fragments and change.

Reflection Questions

1. Think about collage as both provisional coherence and antagonistic cooperation. In what way might collage be imagined as provisional? How do the collage creators endeavour to reach a wider audience and a shared vision (cooperation), and in what ways are there likely to be ongoing tensions according to the topic and/or image (antagonistic)? How might you endeavour to do both from your own subjective point of view?

2. How does this chapter's focus on the arts apply to social innovation? How do you view the connections between art-based and innovative pedagogy? What about between collage-making and acts of resistance, or between collage-making and social innovation?

ACKNOWLEDGEMENTS

This research is supported in part by a Social Sciences and Humanities Research grant, funded by the Government of Canada. All images in this chapter have been reproduced with the permission of their creators.

REFERENCES

Blake, K. (2023). *What kind of collage is that?* Whatapageturner Press.

Bourdieu, P. (1988). Vive la crise! For heterodoxy in social science. *Theory and Society,17*(5), 773–787.

Burgos, M.J. (2020, February 1). Collage art as a form of protest: What artists around the world have to say. *CBC News.* cbc.ca/news/canada/new-brunswick/collage-art-show-unb-1.5445795

Butler, J. (1993). *Bodies that matter: On the discursive limits of "sex."* Routledge.

Butler, J. (2006a). *Gender trouble: Feminism and the subversion of identity.* Routledge.

Butler, J. (2006b). *Precarious life: The powers of mourning and violence.* Verso.

Etgar Y. (2022). On edge: Exploring collage tactics and terminology. In P. Elliott (ed.), *Cut and paste: 400 Years of collage* (pp. 35–49). Scottish National Gallery of Modern Art.

Etgar, Y. (2023). Border control: Testing the limits of collage. In R. Morrill (Ed.), *Vitamin C+, Collage in contemporary art* (pp. 10–17). Phaidon.

Gurney J., & Haladyn, J.J. (2022). *Community of images: Strategies of appropriation in Canadian art, 1977-1990.* YYZBOOKS.

Jordan-Haladyn, M. (2022). Carl Beam, counter-appropriation and polyphonic image text. In J. Gurney, & J.J. Haladyn, (Eds.), *Community of images: Strategies of appropriation in Canadian art, 1977-1990* (pp. 93–110). YYZBOOKS.

Kentridge, W. (2023). World-renowned South African artist William Kentridge on his wide-ranging, politically engaged work. [Radio Interview]. *Writers and Company, CBC Radio.* cbc.ca/listen/live-radio/1-77-writers-and-company/clip/15964239-world-renowned-south-african-artist-william-kentridge-wide-ranging-politically

Kristeva, J. (2002). *Revolt, she said.* (S. Lotringer, Ed., B. Okeefe, Trans.). MIT Press.

Malatjie P. (2023). Openings, Frida Orupabo. *Artforum, 61*(9). www.artforum.com/features/portia/malatjie-on-frida-orupabo-252668/

Moffatt, K. (2019). *Postmodern social work: Reflective practice and education.* Columbia University Press.

Moffatt K. (2021a). A Tribute to R.M. Vaughan: He stirred a cauldron of Canadian craft and culture. *Journal of New Brunswick Studies, 13*(2), 8–15.

Moffatt K. (2021b). Why collage was an ideal artwork for R.M. Vaughan. *Cut Paste Resist Redux.* University of New Brunswick Art Gallery. www.unb.ca/cel/enrichment/art-centre/past-exhibitions/2021-jan-3.html

Moffatt K. (forthcoming). Preface. In A. Davies & C. Greensmith (Eds.), *Queering professionalism: Problems, potential and possibilities in neoliberal times.* University of Toronto Press.

O'Meally, R. G. (2022). *Antagonistic cooperation: Jazz, collage, and the shaping of African American culture.* Columbia University Press.

Simmons, N., & Daley, S. (2013). The art of thinking: Using collage to stimulate scholarly work. *The Canadian Journal for the Scholarship of Teaching and Learning, 4*(1).

Tandon R., Moffatt, K., & Furmli, S. (2021, February 18). *Why collage is an ideal form for resistance.* [Unpublished presentation.] Jack Layton Leadership School, Toronto Metropolitan University.

Vaughan, K. (2005). Pieced together: Collage as an artist's method for interdisciplinary research. *International Journal of Qualitative Methods, 4*(1), 27–52.

The Importance of Justice and Decolonization Questions in Science Education

Brooke Filsinger and Roxana Sühring

> **Learning Objectives**
>
> 1. Understand the "Ethics of Reciprocity" and the responsibility of scientists to land stewardship, as well as to environmental and social justice, using chemists as an example.
> 2. Recognize the importance of identifying and acknowledging personal biases, and of giving consideration to diverse worldviews.
> 3. Comprehend the importance of addressing justice and decolonization questions in science education and how both can influence the role of scientists and their contributions to society.

THE STUDY OF SOCIAL INNOVATION AND SOCIAL JUSTICE is typically associated with the social sciences. However, developments in the natural sciences and engineering substantially impact the fabric of our societies and their priorities for innovation. Moreover, many problems and opportunities created through natural science innovation can cause or address social and environmental justice questions. As such, an argument could be made that questions of social innovation and justice need to be part of natural research and learning. We use the example of chemistry to focus this argument and to provide concrete examples of how questions of justice, decolonization and innovation need to be considered in natural sciences and engineering education.

Chemistry has traditionally been taught as a body of knowledge that builds on the historical discoveries of those deemed to be "important" chemists; and a critique of the fixity and limitations of boundaried, disciplinary knowledges can be seen in Chapter 2. In chemistry, students are expected to transform into chemists by learning a particular body of knowledge and its respective, historical context. Students must learn outdated concepts simply because they are the historical foundation of current knowledge, only to later unlearn information that is neither effective nor pedagogically useful. Recent innovative initiatives in chemistry pedagogy have proposed that chemistry education be approached in a manner where students are taught to think like a chemist rather than focusing on chemistry as a body of knowledge (Talanquer & Pollard, 2010). This paradigm shift prioritizes cognitive skills, problem-solving and a deeper understanding of scientific reasoning over rote memorization of facts and theories. While this shift addresses some of the pedagogical practices of traditional science education, it does not go far enough in addressing very real-world societal implications.

Science, and certainly the field of chemistry, is not isolated from the world it aims to understand and transform; it is a discipline deeply embedded in societal, economic and ethical contexts. Scientists, despite their allegiance to the tenets of scientific objectivity, are not just brains in lab coats; they are individuals shaped by their own cultural, ethical and societal worldviews. This inherently influences not only what questions they choose to investigate, but also how they interpret data, and most critically, how they apply their discoveries. For example, considering the impact that chemical innovation is having on our society — from increased life expectancy due to medical innovations to health crises due to pollution — chemists like other scientists have a unique opportunity (and, we would argue, responsibility) to help address a variety of environmental and social justice questions.

As we face numerous global challenges ranging from climate change and pollution to public health crises, there is a growing need to train scientists such as chemists to be not only skilled at making and manipulating molecules, but also to be capable of grappling with the ethical and justice-oriented questions that their work raises. This transformation necessitates a paradigmatic shift in the sciences, from asking the question of "Could we?" to the far more impactful question of "Should we"?

This chapter is a conversation between Brooke Filsinger, advisor for Indigenous education and decolonization for the Faculty of Science at Toronto Metropolitan University (TMU), and Roxana Sühring, a faculty member in TMU's Department of Chemistry and Biology, whose research and teaching focuses on chemical contaminants and contamination as a justice issue.

INTRODUCTIONS

Roxana: My name is Roxana. I am a German female scientist who moved to Canada a few years ago. I grew up in a household of scientists and environmental activists. During my doctoral research on environmental contaminants, I learned about the outsized impacts of contaminants on Arctic communities — and this was the moment when I realized the interconnectedness of environmental contamination and justice. Since finishing my PhD, I have worked on questions around chemical transport into Arctic communities and other communities that have been impacted without having a say in, or benefit of, the industrial processes that have caused contamination there. As a chemistry educator, I am hoping to make students aware of their power and responsibility toward **environmental stewardship** and its connection to environmental and social justice.

Brooke: Wa'tkonnonwerá:ton. Brooke niyónkyats. Kanyen'kehá:ka niwakonhwentsyò:ten. Ohsweken nitewaké:non nek tsi tkí:teron tsi tkarón:to. My name is Brooke. I am a mixed-raced female of Haudenosaunee and settler ancestry. I was raised outside Community and have been working to find my way back. While conducting provincial health research for nearly two decades, I simultaneously danced and taught my way across **Turtle Island**, Europe and Asia. My experiences within this dance community were instrumental in informing my strong beliefs around social justice education and community-building/caretaking. I returned to academia as a PhD student with a research focus on the inclusion of Indigenous pedagogies and research methodologies in Science, Technology, Engineering and Math (STEM), privileging the Indigenous student experience. While I bring my perspective to my research and the thoughts I share, I speak only for myself.

Given our respective academic positions — faculty member and student/ advisor — it is important to acknowledge that our relationship is subject to the complexities of the power dynamics of the academy's hierarchy between students and professors. However, our relationship was built on friendship long before either of us arrived at the university. We have chosen the ethical stance to view each other reciprocally, as both teacher and student. We draw from our respective expertise and acknowledge the areas where we still have much to learn. We approach this relationship from a place of honesty, vulnerability, humility and partnership. We further acknowledge that we have not come to the understandings and beliefs we discuss in isolation. Our learning journeys have been profoundly enriched by the immense generosity of many, with special acknowledgement to the invaluable contributions of Caleb Wesley, Amy Desjarlais, Alacea Yerxa, Sommerly Grimaldi-Ertl and numerous others among the Indigenous Community at TMU and beyond. We have intentionally included specific individuals in the introduction here, as opposed to in an acknowledgement section at the end, because the learnings in this chapter were heavily influenced by their knowledge-sharing. We do so in an effort to bring Indigenous Knowledges and Oral Tradition practices into academic spaces, even when there is no paper to cite! We are grateful for their support and the wisdom they have generously provided in the past and continue to share with us.

Although presented as a conversation, the following dialogue should not be interpreted merely as a transcription, but rather as a co-constructed reflection based on numerous conversations, interrogations of colonial academic practices, lived observations, shared reflections and collaborative learning over the past two years.

WHY WE NEED TO CONSIDER ETHICS AND SOCIAL JUSTICE IN CHEMISTRY EDUCATION

Roxana: This chapter talks about why it is necessary to teach considerations around ethics and social justice in the sciences, and specifically, in chemistry education. I will start with my perspective as someone who is a chemistry educator, as well as a researcher who works at the interface of chemistry and justice questions.

I would say that chemistry and social justice interface most around contamination in the environment. In fact, I would argue that a significant portion of our current pollution problems might originate from the absence of justice-centric chemistry education. We have graduates who have spent years in chemistry programs and have, at best, taken one course on the ecological consequences of chemical processes. The conversation on potential, unintended consequences of chemical production and use is practically non-existent. So, it is not surprising that questions like potential environmental harm and environmental injustice are not sufficiently considered in most chemical designs.

This lack then leads to a disconnect between the push for more sustainability and the chemical synthesis practices, not just in education but within the discipline of chemistry, in general. For example, perfluorocubane — a per- and polyfluorinated substance (PFAS) — was chosen as "Chemical of the Year 2022" by the American Chemical Society's journal *C&EN* (Krietsch Boerner, 2022), and it is a fascinating molecule. I am sure it is really interesting to think about the synthesis, properties and potential applications. But it belongs to a category of chemicals that environmental chemists and regulators are flagging for their environmental and human health impacts (Cousins et al., 2022). PFAS are of concern because they are highly stable in the environment — sometimes called **forever chemicals**; they are associated with numerous health impacts, like endocrine disruption and cancers; and they are often not effectively removed in water treatment (Cousins et al., 2022). They have fascinating properties though, and are incredibly versatile, which means that, from a synthesis and industry perspective, they are great molecules.

The problem is that the prevailing philosophy in our field is still mostly centred around discovery as the ultimate goal of research. It operates on a principle of "if it is possible, it is worth pursuing," which means that what fascinates us academically ends up overshadowing the urgent issues, like the chemical pollution that we now confront. What we need is a reorientation where we think about potential consequences before making chemicals, and we need to make sure that this change of thinking happens early on in chemistry education. This is why I think it is important to have questions of ethics, impact and justice in a chemistry curriculum and in literature about chemistry education.

Brooke: I am coming at this question from an entirely different perspective in that I haven't been involved specifically with chemistry education in any capacity for many, many years. But I do focus a lot of my time and energy reflecting on creating space for Indigenous Knowledges within STEM education and research, in particular, as well as on approaching education and research from a more holistic perspective, in general. With that noted, I am typically not only considering the physical and mental areas where we tend to focus our energies in academia, I am also concerned about heart and spirit. How do these concerns relate to a scientific field, like chemistry, where traditionally heart and spirit would intentionally not be given any consideration? Are we able to find a more holistic balance?

When I think about social justice in chemistry or chemistry education, I recognize there is an extensive body of knowledge that students are expected to learn. It is not until students are quite advanced in their education that they begin to question or challenge where these knowledges come from. Are these knowledges correct? How have they changed over time? These are questions that students are not allowed to ask until they have already accepted these knowledges and the foundation on which their understanding has been constructed. Maybe I am a contrarian, but I believe there should be the opportunity to start questioning from the very first day, inquiring:

- Who is asking the questions?
- How has this knowledge developed?
- Who has formalized what is "accepted"?

- What knowledge and viewpoints may be missing?
- Have our biases given rise to gaps in thinking that need to be addressed and mitigated?

For me, these are the crucial questions in finding out who decides our accepted bodies of knowledge, what is its genealogy, and who are the knowledge generators. With that said, other important steps, at least in my mind, is to identify our conscious or unconscious biases; position ourselves in our worldview; and understand our personal worldview in relation to others.

EDUCATION, WORLDVIEWS AND THE RESPONSIBILITY OF SCIENCE

Roxana: You've touched upon something incredibly important — the matter of perspectives, and by extension, worldviews. Our current chemistry pedagogy is almost exclusively taught from a **eurocentric** point of view. (Please note that we have intentionally chosen to use lowercase for "eurocentric" in an effort toward rebalancing the authority of Indigenous [and other] Knowledges.) It is as though the foundational texts and principles we teach are filtered through one specific, cultural lens and conveyed as absolute truths. It is a paradox, really, considering that later in their education, students are introduced to the idea that there is no such thing as an absolute truth. But what happens is that the eurocentric perspective is implicitly enforced as the canonical truth, and, in so doing, alternative ways of knowing — be they biocentric, holistic or ecocentric — are marginalized. Imagine what would happen if students were exposed to these diverse perspectives from the onset. Wouldn't that invariably shape how they approach chemical research and development?

Brooke: I think that's a really important consideration! It is not necessarily detrimental to have personal biases or individualized worldviews, so long as we can identify what they are and appropriately address the potential gaps in our thinking. Understanding our worldview helps us to frame how we approach and understand research — our conclusions and interpretations — and what we do with these findings. All of which leads us to the conversation around the idea of objectivity or pseudo-objectivity. As scientists, we're trained to be so-called objective observers. Neutral. Impartial. Uninfluenced by our biases, emotions and preconceived notions. In practice, we each bring different knowledges, experiences and beliefs to our work. Even though students and scientists are taught to be objective in methodologies, analyses and conclusions, none of us can truly be objective.

At best, we employ pseudo-objectivity. This understanding should always inform our work and interpretations, but it is rarely acknowledged.

Roxana: We have talked about this previously, and again I think this is such an important point — objectivity and the lack of objectivity. The questions we pose and the intellectual lenses through which we view the world shape the conclusions at which we arrive.

As a student, I had a great exercise in my second year, which highlighted this point. We were given two papers on the exact same topic — one written by environmental advocates and the other, by industry. Despite using virtually identical data sets, the conclusions the authors arrived at were completely different. That experience really exposed the inherent subjectivity in data interpretation and shaped my way of reading scientific literature.

This discussion ties back to our point about worldviews, but also to another important point that I have been reflecting on a lot: the responsibilities we have as scientists. I would argue that there's the universal, human responsibility to be stewards of the Earth. But there is an added layer of obligation for us as scientists living within treaty territories. The treaties obligate us to share the land, to leave something behind, to keep it clean and to only take what we need (Loft, 2021). When we understand ourselves as part of, or guests upon, these treaty lands, we should ask ourselves what these treaty obligations mean if we are, for example, making, researching or using chemicals. The exploration and understanding of diverse, and particularly Indigenous, worldviews are not just something that is "nice to have." It is not something to simply make us a more critical thinker. It is how we honour and abide by our treaty obligations.

CRITICAL THINKING

Brooke: This point around treaty obligations is so important. And I am glad you also raised the idea of critical thinking. Often critical thinking, a crucial cognitive skill that must be developed and requires practice, is overlooked or is one of the last things taught in science education. I had a recent conversation with one of our Indigenous students who was questioning why critical thinking is only taught in undergraduate fourth year and only in particular programs within our faculty. They believed, as do I, that these concepts should be presented much, much earlier in their education.

By the time students get to fourth year, a lot of their ideas are fully formed, and they've already accepted one particular way of verifying "truth." But there are students, Indigenous and others, who are potentially starting a postsecondary education with a completely different worldview and understanding of science — what science is, and ways of generating knowledge, understanding and relationships to the world. In the case of Indigenous students specifically, they often are already understanding and upholding treaties that are not being upheld on the other side. So, when these students, with different worldviews, enter a postsecondary institution, they're being asked to learn and to accept knowledges that they potentially have been questioning from day one. The other students, on the other hand, may not even realize that they can question this knowledge and that they can ask where the knowledge is coming from. And perhaps even more importantly, that they can look at the knowledge generators and can question their **positionality**.

I recently taught a graduate course where we discussed the idea of positionality — stating who you are and what you are about. What do you bring to the science? How do you understand your role and your position? What do you want me to know about you? This was a really radical concept for a lot of graduate students — science students — to have to state their position in relation to their work, whereas I would argue that it is fundamental to understanding how you got to the place that you got: your research methods, your research question, your analysis interpretation, how you're choosing to approach future work, all of these matters link integrally back to your positionality as a person. And so, in understanding your positionality, I can understand your work. But in removing that positionality, you remove such an important piece of my ability to understand and relate to this body of research that you're producing and disseminating.

Roxana: Absolutely. Your point on critical thinking and our place in science education is so important. It is fascinating, is it not, how critical thinking as a skill — crucial for any scientist — is often treated as almost an afterthought or something that you will "pick up" during your studies? While undergraduates are, in an ideal world, trained to find and interpret scientific literature, they are not taught to identify biases. It is somewhat paradoxical, considering that any scientist does precisely that: gauges the reliability of a study by assessing affiliations, previous research and other such factors that could potentially introduce bias. This ties into your point on positionality. The supposed objectivity in science demands a researcher to separate themselves from their work as though their personal, social and ethical perspectives were contaminants rather than assets. This is ridiculous. After all, we are inseparable from our thoughts, lived experiences, cognitive frameworks and ethical compasses. So how can we identify biases if we ignore ourselves and others as parts of the interpretation of our research?

This also circles back to our earlier conversation on social justice. If scientists were encouraged and trained to bring their full selves into their research, their work would probably be more ethical and socially aware. I believe that it would naturally prompt us to consider the broader implications and consequences of our work.

The other point you touched on that I believe is critical is the disempowerment of students in an academic setting that only presents one way of seeing the world and generating knowledge. This power dynamic, through how the material is presented but also through grading, for example, effectively quashes any critical thinking. It is a problem that we, as educators and researchers, must address if we want to educate more reflective, critical and just scientists. In this collection, Chapter 6 offers examples of innovative pedagogical practices that could enrich critical thinking toward social transformation.

RELATIONSHIP IN SCIENCE AND
THE NEED FOR LESS OBJECTIVITY

Brooke: I agree; and I would argue that even though some would give lip service to the idea that students can challenge professors, in reality, it is generally not encouraged or practised. There is still very much that dynamic of "I convey the information and you accept the information." This is perpetuated by the way that science education is practised. Much of the time, at least when I was a student, it was one-way learning — basically, an information dump. And if you do take it away and question it or sit with it or find limitations in its thinking, there's rarely, if ever, that opportunity to have a more fulsome discussion because it is always on to the next concept. So even if, from a professor's perspective, they are open to that opportunity for students to dialogue, challenge or question, this dialogue, in practice, is not really given the time or space that would be needed to develop this skill. Because it really is a skill that needs to be developed and practised by students. And again, I think a lot of the onus is put on students to understand that they can do this type of questioning work and to do it themselves — to create the time and space themselves to develop these critical skills that they probably do not even recognize as being important; and really a lot of students just do not have the time nor the energy to do it, especially when it is not given priority.

One of the other things you were talking about, to which I want to return, is our relationship to our research. I am always thinking about relationship. From my particular worldview, when I am thinking about research, I am really thinking about trying to understand whatever it is I am researching by being in relation with it. So, the more relationship I have or the closer I can get to whatever I am trying to understand, the better my understanding will be. I think that's a piece that's also missing from a lot of education: that relationship with each other, with our professors, with the academy, with the land. We try to remove that idea even though we inherently are in some sort of relationship. If we're not caretaking that relationship and understanding that it is a relationship, then things have the potential to go downhill really quickly. There's the possibility for imbalance, misunderstanding, and the potential to develop these skewed views about power and power dynamics. You can ask questions, for instance, but what questions should you ask?

Roxana: Exactly. I love your point on relationships not only with each other, but with the things we research, our institutions, the land and the community that this research will impact. But that is in such stark contrast to the idea that "good scientists" should take themselves out of their research. This idea of pseudo-objectivity, where we are led to believe that the mind can function in isolation, it is incredible how pervasive this idea is. I mean, neuroscience itself would counter such a reductionist view. Our frontal cortex is not operating in a vacuum, separate from our emotions or social context. Max Weber argued as early as 1904 that there is no science free of value, judgment and personal perspective by the researcher (Goddard, 1973), but the contrary argument is still stubbornly made.

Speaking of context, let's talk about the elephant in the room: academic evaluation. Our current grading system sets up the professor as a sort of gatekeeper, doesn't it? Students are not just navigating the material; they are also navigating the power dynamics in academia. If the endgame becomes about securing that "A," what room is left for meaningful critical thought and learning? It really worries me. We're in institutions that are supposed to foster intellectual curiosity and critical thinking, but grading metrics and other academic, hierarchical structures, including "hidden curricula," end up stifling those very attributes. Students become risk-averse, not because they don't want to put the effort in, but because the system incentivizes a certain form of academic conformity. It is as if we are teaching them that the ultimate prize is not understanding but rather a certificate that symbolizes it. So, in essence, the academy runs the risk of becoming transactional, when what we need is a more relational, even transformational, educational model.

MOVING FROM "CAN WE?" TO "SHOULD WE?"

Brooke: Just as you were talking, I was also recognizing that long-time tenured professors, and those who have been in their respective fields for quite some time, are potentially disadvantaged in that they have built this whole body of knowledge and understanding without ever having to consider other viewpoints, without ever having to reconcile the idea of pseudo-objectivity, biases and bringing their worldviews to their work. They are not necessarily equipped with these skills either; and, it could potentially be quite daunting to be challenged, which I think disincentivizes professors to shift their work and thinking. Working in this way does require more thought, more thinking, more reflection and more self-evaluation; and again, there's not necessarily always the time, the space and the willingness to do that, particularly within the constraints of a postsecondary education or institution.

Roxana: Yes! And that brings us back to how the way we see chemical research is tied to what society thinks is important. The problem is that the focus is on "What can be done?" rather than the crucial question of "What should be done?" So, then the question is "How can we shift chemistry education to instill also a strong sense of social responsibility?" We owe it to our students, and the communities they'll eventually impact, to equip them with the tools that they'll need to question, challenge and ultimately change the way things are. So how do we create a curriculum that goes beyond mere mentions of ethics and social concerns and embeds these issues into the core of how we teach and understand chemistry? This would mean teaching them that, as chemists, our job is not "just" to ask whether a new molecule can be made, but also what the broader impact of that molecule would be on public health, social equity, environmental sustainability and even global politics. That would mean a change not just in the curriculum but in the entire academic culture, which would make a lot of people very uncomfortable, as you said. It would basically challenge what it commonly means to be "a chemist" or "a scientist."

Brooke: And from my perspective, coming from both my worldview but also my background and work in public health research, it absolutely blows my mind that these questions are not being asked! And that there is no consideration around the situation of "I can make this molecule, but should I?" How is it not front of mind to consider the impacts of making these molecules? What are the long-term impacts, not only on me and my environment, but the environment of my children and my children's children? Will these molecules still be impacting things down the road?

Particularly when we have examples of exactly this happening. Things we created thirty, forty, fifty, eighty years ago are still impacting our health and our environment today, and our capacity to create has since exponentially increased. And with that, so has our capacity to choose to do harm or choose to do good. It really does blow my mind that these questions are not the first questions that are being asked. That is not to say that we cannot be curious, that we cannot be curiosity-driven, but I think that there is a responsibility to have these considerations along with that curiosity.

Roxana: Yeah, I absolutely agree, and I think that this is such a fundamental point of why we need to talk about this matter, and why it is so important to re-evaluate how we teach chemistry, in general. It is so strange that the ethical dimensions of chemistry are only talked about in graduate studies or toward the very end of undergraduate education — if it gets talked about at all. We should teach a sense of social and environmental stewardship from the moment we start introducing students to chemistry in high school. It would be so impactful if we educated young students on the benefits, as well as the risks, of chemical innovation. That would mean that we are educating critical thinkers who know how important it is to ask not just how, but why, and at what cost. There have been some recent publications where this issue is being discussed: for example, conversations around the need to raise "essential use" as a concept when thinking about chemical registration and regulation (Figuiere et al., 2023). This means that the question of "Do we need it?" is finally being considered rather than just the question of possibility, or even, profitability. Another recent paper argued that the chemical industry and chemical research have to change to make sure that modern chemistry is not "rubbish" (Flerlage & Slootweg, 2023).

Brooke: Oh, amazing!

Roxana: Yeah. "Modern Chemistry is Rubbish" is literally the title of the publication. Unfortunately, these issues are discussed by a narrow group of environmental chemists and environmental scientists who work on pollution issues. The "Molecule of the Year" that we talked about earlier exemplifies this paradox. How can we laud a PFAS compound when its potential ecological impacts are so horrendous (Cousins et al., 2022)? We have been advocating for PFAS restrictions; and PFAS have been the subject of intense scrutiny and regulatory debate (EPA, 2021). To celebrate it is like patting ourselves on the back for causing maximum ecological harm.

But again, the questions are "What can we do about this?" and "How do we reconcile sustainability, curiosity-driven chemistry research and a profit-driven chemical industry?" From the days of the alchemists, chemistry

138 INTERRUPTING INNOVATION

has been trying to understand natural phenomena and advancing materials, human well-being and our knowledge. Questions of "What can be made?" and "How can it be improved?" have driven the field. But the question has rarely been: "Just because I can, should I?"

MOVING SCIENCE OUT OF THE VACUUM

Brooke: I think for me it all goes back to this question: "Are we doing science in a vacuum?" Also, "Are we teaching science only in the lab? Or, are we throwing out that idea of objectivity and moving toward an understanding of our place in relation to the world in which we live?" If we understand that everything we do has an impact on our environment and our relationships, then I think we understand that it is not just a molecule that I've created in a vacuum and it is really incredible. It is that this molecule has real impact, or at least has the potential to have real impacts, and with that I have a responsibility, to the best of my ability, to ensure that those are not harmful impacts. I have a responsibility to myself and to my relations, be those my human relations or the non-human beings inhabiting this planet, to consider the potential impacts of this molecule I've created, and to ask whether they are greater than any potential benefits. Are there long-term impacts? That is, is this molecule going to create problems?

With the way that science is currently taught, for the most part, it is very easy to separate ourselves from these incredibly important considerations. We recognize all the previous, amazing discoveries and the dreams of discoveries still to come, and we build on the foundation. And we only briefly educate without fully understanding (or commonly, not even acknowledging), the negative impacts of these scientific discoveries. But when we understand that we don't operate in a vacuum and that everything we do has an impact, I think it is a lot harder to flippantly create molecules or create chemicals or have a PFAS be the molecule of the year. Because we understand that there are real-world, long-term, significant impacts. So, for me, it really goes back to the idea of being in relation, not only with the knowledge, but with what that knowledge is producing.

Roxana: This reminds me of a quote I heard recently from Jerry Daniels, Grand Chief of the Southern Chiefs' Organization in Manitoba. I thought what he said really illustrated the importance of relationship and understanding of our different worldviews. He said that reconciliation, from his perspective, is reconciling an Indigenous worldview with the worldviews of Canadians and newcomers because right now, there is a disconnect between these worldviews—particularly when it comes to treaty rights and treaty responsibilities. From an Indigenous perspective, there is respect that is given to the land and the water as they are part of relationships and kin, whereas science typically sees the land and water as a commodity that can be used, extracted and transformed into whatever suits the needs of some. As people living on treaty lands, we should learn and teach about the personhood of the land and water and that we are infringing on their rights as beings when we make chemicals that will pollute them. If we consider this definition of reconciliation, then pollution stands directly in the way of reconciling.

Brooke: I think it is a really important point. If you look at land or water or plants or animals as a commodity, then you treat them, understand them and respect them a certain way — or don't respect them. Alternatively, if you consider these entities as beings that share this space with you, then you have a much different relationship with them than you would to a commodity. And were you to further shift your perspective or understanding to consider these beings as gifting themselves to sustain you, how would that further shift your thinking from a commodity mindset? It brings a much greater respect to that relationship.

We, as humans and scientists, have such great capacity for creation. But with that capacity, are we considering our interconnectedness, our ethical awareness and our responsibility to be in good relation with our environment? Are we minimizing our impacts? Are we operating in sustainable ways? What are we giving back to our environment? Incorporating reciprocity into chemistry, chemistry education and environmental stewardship emphasizes the importance of ethical and sustainable practices. We recognize that our actions have consequences that have the potential to impact not only our environment but also that of future generations, for better or for worse.

We need to intentionally make and hold space in science for other perspectives and worldviews. And I think there are different ways to think about that, right? You can look to Two-Eyed Seeing and weaving Indigenous and eurocentric Knowledges (Bartlett & Marshall, 2012). You can look to **Two-Row Wampum** and Knowledges that are travelling side-by-side (Hill & Coleman, 2018). Those from other Nations and cultures will have their own teachings that they can bring to the table. We all have our own lived experiences and personal worldviews that can and should contribute to our collective understanding. I believe it is not important that we all have the same teachings or perspectives, but rather that we're making space for all these Knowledges to coexist with respectful understanding of each other.

CONCLUSION

This chapter has explored the multi-faceted dimensions of science education and research. Giving examples from chemistry education, we focused on the often-overlooked areas of ethics, social justice and environmental responsibility. We hoped to have highlighted the critical gaps in current, pedagogical models and the imperative need for a paradigmatic shift.

Drawing upon divergent backgrounds — one rooted in traditional chemistry education and the other in Indigenous Knowledge systems (Absolon, 2022) — we have arrived at a consensus that a reformed approach to science education is essential. Science education needs an integrated curriculum that does not treat ethical considerations, social justice and environmental impact as supplementary elements, but rather as foundational to scientific inquiry. Another important point is the limitations of the eurocentric approach to science education. Instead, we propose a pluralistic model that accommodates different ways of knowing and alternative paradigms such as biocentrism, holism and ecocentrism. This change includes questioning the fallacy of objectivity in scientific research, and acknowledging that the interpretation of data is inextricably linked to the researcher's own biases, experiences and worldviews. Allowing for these different perspectives enables a student's early introduction to critical thinking and ethical considerations in their educational journey.

Considering the multitude of environmental pollution and justice issues that we face, it is important that we rethink science education to be more holistic, ethically grounded and socially responsible. We contend that such a transformation is not just an academic exercise, but a moral obligation, especially in the context of global challenges that require interdisciplinary and cross-cultural collaboration for sustainable solutions.

Reflection Questions

1. How can educational institutions implement a curriculum that integrates ethics, social justice and environmental considerations from the outset, rather than treating them as supplementary topics? What challenges might they encounter in this process, and how could they be overcome?

2. In what ways can researchers and educators acknowledge and navigate their own biases, positionality and worldviews to conduct more equitable and responsible science? How might this change the landscape of scientific research and its societal impact?

3. How can Western scientific paradigms be reconciled with Indigenous worldviews, especially in the context of environmental stewardship and social justice? What models or frameworks, such as Two-Eyed Seeing or Two-Row Wampum, might facilitate this integration, and what would be the implications for both academic and community-based research?

REFERENCES

Absolon, K. E. (2022). *Kaandossiwin: How we come to know: Indigenous research methodologies* (2nd ed.). Fernwood Publishing.

Bartlett, C., Marshall, M., & Marshall, A. (2012). Two-Eyed Seeing and other lessons learned within a co-learning journey of bringing together Indigenous and mainstream knowledges and ways of knowing. *Journal of Environmental Studies and Sciences, 2*(4), 331–340.

Cousins, I.T., Johansson, J.H, Salter, M.E., Sha, B., & Scheringer, M. (2022). Outside the safe operating space of a new planetary boundary for per- and polyfluoroalkyl substances (PFAS). *Environmental Science & Technology, 56*(16), 11172–11179.

Figuière, R., Borchert, F., Cousins, I.T., & Agerstrand, M. (2023). The essential-use concept: A valuable tool to guide decision-making on applications for authorisation under REACH? *Environmental Sciences Europe, 35*(5), 1-12.

Flerlage, H., & Slootweg, J.C. (2023). Modern chemistry is rubbish. *Nature Reviews Chemistry, 7*(9), 593–594.

Goddard, D. (1973). Max Weber and the objectivity of social science. *History and Theory, 12*(1), 1–22.

Hill, R.W., & Coleman, D. (2019). The Two Row Wampum–Covenant Chain tradition as a guide for Indigenous–university research partnerships. *Cultural Studies ↔ Critical Methodologies, 19*(5), 339–359.

Krietsch Boerner, L. (2022). Molecules of the year. *Chemical & Engineering News, 100*(44), 32–33.

Loft, A. (2021). Remember like we do. In D. Bolduc, M. Gordon-Corbiere, R., Tabobondung, & B. Wright-McLeod (Eds.), *Indigenous Toronto: Stories that carry this place* (pp. 17–28). Coach House Books.

Talanquer,V., & Pollard, J. (2010). Let's teach how we think instead of what we know. *Chemistry Education Research and Practice, 11*(2), 74–83.

United States Environmental Protection Agency. (2021). *Key EPA actions to address PFAS.* United States Environmental Protection Agency. www.epa.gov/pfas/key-epa-actions-address-pfas.

Innovate for Impact

Unleashing Social Change through Values-Driven Leadership and Visionary Action

Wilson Leung

> **Learning Objectives**
> 1. Discovering our core values and crafting our leadership purpose.
> 2. Identifying societal challenges and creating a vision for change.
> 3. Turning vision into action.

UP TO THIS POINT IN OUR LEARNING, we have been conceptualizing social innovation by studying key concepts and theoretical reflections. We have also been examining case examples to better grasp these conceptualizations through a social justice lens and building knowledge to tackle systemic issues. Learning theories of social innovation and concepts of social justice are certainly important. However, learning these theories themselves are not the goal. Rather, making the world a better place is the ultimate goal. As we increase our knowledge of key concepts, it is also important that we consider the practical and hands-on methods to support our learning journey toward social activism. This is important so we can move from learning about social issues to putting into action our contributions to social transformation. It will be essential to not merely learn about the various theories of social justice but also to personally experience what it means for us to become positive leaders for social change.

Moreover, reflections and engagements with social innovation have impact beyond the bounds of the classroom or academic settings. Some of us may be students in higher education, while others may come from various backgrounds and walks of life. Know that these social innovation learnings can and should be adapted to the various contexts and settings where we find ourselves. Together, we can have a much greater influence as positive change agents for humanity.

This chapter develops a deeper understanding of our values and leadership purpose that will be foundational to a vision for positive societal change. We will gain a greater sense of self-awareness in regard to our own beliefs and convictions, culminating in the articulation of our personal sense of purpose. This purpose informs a more focused leadership perspective and supports the identification of a societal challenge. Out of this greater societal need, a vision is born. This vision then flows into practices of experimentation and implementation to bring the social innovation into reality. The chapter ends with exploring applications from a case study of a graduate experiential learning program for social innovation.

We are invited to fully engage in this chapter's journey. Try not to read this chapter only from an academic perspective, but also from a lens of personal reflection and application. By only viewing the learning from an educational standpoint, we may gain some knowledge but miss the more essential aspects of personal and societal transformation. Wishing each reader a wonderful adventure as we explore together what it means to engage in this transformation!

DISCOVERING OUR CORE VALUES

Whether we are walking, biking, driving or commuting, we may have navigated somewhere before. There are two essential tools for navigation: a map and a compass. Both seem somewhat similar as tools to help us get to where we need to go. Yet, a map and compass also have distinctive features.

A map is detailed and precise. When we use the map app on our devices and select our destination, we are provided with an estimate of the minutes and hours it will take to arrive, along with an accurate distance calculation. On the contrary, a compass is much less detailed; it will not provide an estimated time of arrival nor calculate how far our destination will be. We might wonder what a compass is good for! Well, a compass will tell us if we are heading in the right direction, and orient us to where we currently are and the direction we want to go.

As we navigate through life and leadership challenges, we may wish we had an imaginary map. Instead, we have access to another kind of tool that helps us guide our life plans and motivations for social innovation impact: we have an internal compass of our core, personal values which inform us whether we are progressing toward the social innovation purposes that are most meaningful and aligned with us. Cashman (2017) describes how we tend to place too much emphasis on the what and how of life, yet we overlook the why.

Our values indicate what is most significant to us and are the seeds through which we discover our purpose – "the why." The values we hold will be significant and meaningful to us personally and will guide our subsequent actions. What specific values are meaningful to us? What values are most important to us and why? We may already have certain values that come to mind. For those of us who may be unsure of our values, try doing an internet search of various lists of values to consider — for example, see Brown (2023) for a list of 117 values to consider.

We can reflect on our values by asking key questions such as: Why is this value meaningful or worthwhile to us? How is this value demonstrated in our lives? What are the ways in which this value is expressed? When was the last time we experienced this value in a significant way?

How would we react if this value was challenged or taken from us?

As we contemplate our response to these questions, our values of highest priority will emerge. As they do, we can allow these values to begin shaping our internal compass, thereby giving us a sense of direction, a social-justice purpose.

Brown (2023) challenges us to not only articulate our values but also to find applications for them in our lives. It is not enough to just be aware of our values; it's essential to put them into action. Life is more meaningful when what we think, say and do intentionally matches our attitudes and beliefs. Why is it important to translate our values from awareness into behaviours? One reason is sheer practicality. Life is busy in multiple facets, whether that is with our education, our career, our family or other personal commitments. We need to be discerning with how we spend our time and energy.

Another reason why it is essential to align our values with actions is because, in the absence of that, there will likely be a lack of meaning and fulfilment in our lives. We may start feeling aimless or frustrated with our inability to conduct our lives in ways that we truly believe. Covey (2020) insightfully challenges readers to form the habit of beginning with the end in mind. It is crucial to consider our long-term, life priorities rather than merely focusing on short-term, daily demands. These long-term goals are supported by an intentional mindset of consistently applying our core values to day-to-day decisions. As we build this habit of applying our values consistently over extended periods of time, we will begin to experience a greater sense of meaning and personal satisfaction.

> ## Reflection Questions
>
> Before reading the next section, take some time to reflect on these questions:
>
> 1. What are your top five values? Why are these values important to you?
> 2. Given the top values that you have selected, what approaches could help you to more consistently put your values into action?
> 3. How could your values be used as an internal compass to provide life direction for you?

CRAFTING OUR LEADERSHIP PURPOSE

As we discover our core values and consistently integrate them into our lives, this internal compass will help give us a sense of direction. That said, it is important to not only have a direction, but to have a destination in mind. This brings us to purpose. If uncovering our values is like knowing our direction, then understanding our purpose is like knowing our destination. Renshaw (2018) describes purpose as the source of one's existence that motivates and challenges us toward some form of action. The author then goes on to outline various benefits of having purpose, such as creating a sense of meaning. This meaning is relevant in one's life as it allows an individual to grow and reach their potential. Having purpose inspires us toward action and provides us with a deeper level of personal fulfilment and significance. Knowing both our values and our purpose establishes a foundation upon which we begin building a vision for social innovation.

Cashman (2017) goes even further, aligning purpose with mastery. It is not just about leading "with" purpose but also leading "on" purpose. There is both a heightened awareness of the importance of having purpose but also an increased level of intentionality to lead purposefully. To achieve anything of mastery requires dedication, effort, practice and sacrifice. Learning to lead with purpose is an acquired skill that is no different. The more strategic we are about leading with purpose, the more we will excel at it. Some of us may have opportunities to lead with purpose in an academic setting, while others may find themselves in various life arenas where they can lead with intentionality. Regardless of our setting, let us be committed to leading and being positive leaders for humanity.

But what does it even mean to lead? What is leadership? These may seem like straightforward questions, yet our response to them will be a significant determinant of our purpose. People will define leadership and the purpose of it differently. Some leverage leadership to see what they can gain from it.

146 INTERRUPTING INNOVATION

They lead in a manner that benefits themselves in a self-serving way. Some believe leadership is a matter of having power or authority over others. Scott (2019) notes the difference between a leader and a tyrant. A leader will work hard to serve others, whereas a tyrant will use their authority to make others serve them. This is one end of the leadership spectrum.

The other end of the continuum views leadership not as being about how we can gain, but about how others can benefit. To lead with purpose is about how we can serve and help others. Keyser (2019) explains the principle of selfless service as being less concerned about ourselves and having greater consideration for the well-being of those around us. Falke (2022) highlights that one of the important pillars of leading well is to give back. As a leader focuses on giving rather than taking, they make a positive difference in the world and attain a healthier perspective of life's priorities.

Now, it is imperative to articulate our leadership purpose. The purpose statement we create will be brief, possibly only a sentence or two. The benefit of a short one is that it will be memorable for us to recall whenever we wish to reflect on it. It is important to review and connect our values to form some kind of guiding concept or overarching principle. To support the crafting of a purpose statement, it is helpful to not only embrace our values, but to consider several other additional aspects. We can begin by thinking about mentors whom we may have had who have had significant influence on our lives. If we have never had a mentor before, consider other positive figures, such as a parent, sibling, friend, teacher, neighbour, classmate or colleague. It would be helpful to process what qualities we admire about them or the traits that we highly respect in them and that we wish to emulate in our own lives.

Next, we can examine the chapters that make up our lives, thinking of our lives as a book made up of different sections. We can note the various chapter themes and nuances that we have experienced; and we can be grateful for the successes, joys and victories that have made us who we are today, as well as recognize the positive, defining moments of our lives. We also need to take time to acknowledge our low points, including failures, disappointments, setbacks and regrets. Despite these being more negative elements in our lives, we can still ask ourselves what insights or lessons we can glean from them.

Then, it is helpful to take time to create a life map for ourselves. So, what is a life map? It can be defined as "a visual diagram that represents a person's past, present and future. This diagram is a graphic organizer that helps individuals reflect on key moments in their lives, set goals and plan for the future" (see www.mindomo.com/blog/life-map/). This website also provides further instructions, tools and templates on how to design a life map.

Finally, connecting values, mentors, life chapters and our life map will help us synthesize all these elements into a leadership-purpose statement. It is helpful to make this statement as meaningful and memorable as possible, as the goal is to recall it often in moment-to-moment situations, circumstances and decisions of our daily life. On the Happier Human website, one can find the story, "37 Personal Purpose Statement Examples and Ideas for 2023," which includes a variety of purpose statements, provides details on how to create a purpose statement and gives the benefits of doing so (see www. happierhuman.com/personal-purpose-statements/).

Reflection Questions

Before reading the next section, take some time to reflect on these questions:

1. Who are the mentors who have influenced you? How so?
2. Which chapters in your life are the defining ones? Why is that?
3. What is your leadership purpose statement? Can you memorize it?

IDENTIFYING SOCIETAL CHALLENGES

In the last couple of sections, we learned that uncovering our values gives us a sense of direction and that understanding our leadership purpose provides clarity of destination. This section now shifts the focus outwardly to consider the world of challenges all around us. Whether we are watching the news, receiving a smartphone notification or reading about social justice issues across the country, there is certainly no shortage of global problems or complexities to overcome.

Emmaline Soken-Huberty, a writer for "Human Rights Careers," identifies the "Top 20 Current Global Issues We Must Address," which include challenges such as poverty, children's rights, climate change, food insecurity, refugee rights, health care, mental health, disability rights and gender equality (see: www.humanrightscareers.com/issues/current-global-issues/). Perhaps we can even think of other global issues that come to mind. At the same time, societal challenges do not just occur only on a global scale. We may be aware of social justice needs locally that are happening in our own city, community or neighbourhood. The main point is that there are many social justice needs, so we need to consider how we might begin to align them with our core values and leadership purpose.

The challenges happening either locally or globally can feel so daunting. The thought of how to go about tackling these issues is certainly overwhelming. Before beginning to tackle the societal challenges, though, we must begin with a bigger hurdle: our mindset. The extent to which we can shift our own perspective about these local and global problems will likely influence the extent to which we can actually have an impact. Tom Peterson outlines the skill of reframing, noting that "before you spend energy looking for answers, make sure you have a question worth asking. [...] To reframe, step back and look at a situation from different angles, in different lights, through different lenses" (see: www.thunderheadworks. com/ten-ways-reframe-problem-challenge/). Peterson continues to describe reframing techniques, such as: flipping a challenge from negative to positive; thinking of a better question; breaking down the big challenge into a series of smaller challenges; and looking at the bigger picture.

As we start to reframe the various global or local challenges as possibilities, we can start asking ourselves where our passion lies. This is important because there will always be many more problems in the world than our capacity to solve. Kouzes and Posner (2017) describe how there is greater difficulty creating possibilities when there is a lack of passion. We need to connect with our feelings and emotions to envision the future. These authors go on to advise that setbacks and sacrifices are inevitable, making it even more essential to align with the societal need that is most important to us.

To help with determining what is most important to us, we can reflect upon which societal problems inspire us to experience the greatest levels of empathy. Lockwood and Papke (2018) describe empathy as putting ourselves into someone else's situation so that we can identify and relate to how they feel. The authors go on to highlight how empathy is the foundation for innovation and creativity. What global or local challenges do we most empathize with? Determining this will help us assess what societal issues are most meaningful to us and may help unleash exciting ideas for innovation and creativity as solutions.

Reflection Questions

Before reading the next section, take some time to reflect on these questions:

1. Review the list of global issues indicated above or think of other global and local issues not listed. Which social justice issues do you have the most passion for? Why is that?
2. How would you describe your level of empathy for this societal problem?
3. How might you reframe this seemingly daunting societal challenge into a more productive mindset toward it?

CREATING A VISION FOR CHANGE

The word "vision" is often associated with a company or business wishing to describe a future state of what that organization wants to become. Yet, we do not often think of vision when it comes to our personal lives and the impact that we want to make in the world. Vision involves our imagination and is future-oriented. Vision focuses on the big picture and considers long-term goals and objectives. Stanley (2023) describes how vision is a goal we aim for and a future outcome that we strive toward. There exists a significant gap between the current reality and this future-oriented vision, so it requires taking risks and actions in order to bring vision to life.

Those visions that seem larger-than-life are often the most exciting. Herold (2018) describes how plans that are too small and safe usually do not motivate or influence. Bigger visions typically provide a greater sense of purpose, meaning and inspiration. Herold goes on to explain how coming up with an effective vision requires us to put into practice some childlike dreaming to unlock the playful parts of our brains. Some of us were likely more inventive and creative in our childhood, now trying as adults to be more realistic and pragmatic. Think about the global or local challenges in the previous section that we have passion and empathy for. What vision for positive change might we have? What mental image might we have of future possibilities that could help support that societal need? How could we be innovative or creative about future opportunities to help solve this social justice challenge?

As we explore these personal vision questions, it is also helpful to root our responses with the themes from the previous sections. Try to root our vision by combining earlier insights that we may have had. For example, reflect on how our core values and leadership purpose statement could synthesize with our vision for positive change. Consider how our passion and empathy for a specific societal problem speak to our future-oriented vision for that issue.

Vision is essentially comprised of two individual, yet integrated, components. The first is a mental image of imagination and innovation that we previously learned. Yet, vision is more than just a creative picture in our minds. It also involves an equally crucial element: our hearts. For a vision to be compelling, it not only taps into a creative sense of innovation, but it also connects with a sense of conviction and belief. We may even feel like our vision is a moral obligation to fulfil, a sense of calling to pursue throughout our lives.

As a personal activity, we can try incorporating Brown's (2023) list of values and Kristensen's (2023) examples of purpose statements mentioned above. For example, we can contemplate what it could mean to tackle a local community issue of poverty if our top five values are "compassion, justice, future generations, courage and inclusion" and our purpose statement is "Empowering marginalized young men by giving them the resources they need to overcome racial, educational, political and socio-economic barriers and injustices." Or we can imagine what we could do for the global issue of children's rights if our values are "ethics, equality, giving back, fairness and service" and our purpose statement is "Serving in a role where we identify the most vulnerable, and work to bring them resources that will help them gain physiological security." The point is to not only think about a solution for a societal problem, but to harness that solution from the deep and meaningful set of convictions and beliefs that resonate with us.

We learned earlier that grander visions inspire people more than safe and small plans. When it comes to moving forward with our vision, however, think small. It may be intimidating to think about all the components that we may not yet have in place, such as resources (a budget, volunteers and partnerships). Spodek (2019) encourages us to start where we are with what we have and leverage it, even if it feels seemingly insignificant. Perhaps it is a local, non-profit organization where we can begin asking some questions. Perhaps it is a friend or family member with whom we can share our ideas. Perhaps we have some free time to volunteer at a community charity. It is important to not overthink it, but to just get started.

To start something means taking initiative. Spodek (2019) continues to describe the Initiative-Action-Passion cycle. The concept of this cycle is that as we go ahead to take initiative, action will begin happening, which will then generate more passion within us. As more passion grows within us, it triggers more initiative, and the cycle continues.

It is not about worrying whether or not we are making a big, positive change. It is about focusing on making any positive change. We don't focus on whether we see substantial progress; we focus on any progress, knowing that even with small steps, we are still making a positive difference that helps to impact positively that societal need.

> ## Reflection Questions
> Before reading the next section, take some time to reflect on these questions:
> 1. What mental image of future possibilities could help solve a global or local societal challenge?
> 2. How do your values and your leadership purpose statement align with this societal challenge?
> 3. Considering where you are and what you have to work with, what could you do to get started?

TURNING VISION INTO ACTION

At this point in our social innovation journey, it is time to pull our learning together. We have discovered our top values that serve as an internal compass and considered approaches to consistently put these values into action. We have reflected on our defining moment and the mentors who have influenced us, and we have crafted our leadership purpose statement. We have identified and reframed a societal challenge for which we have passion and empathy. We have also thought about a vision of future possibilities and encouraged ourselves to start where we are with what we have.

The next step is to integrate this learning and turn it into action. We do this through experimentation. We will not know if something works unless we try it out. Swoboda (2020) describes what it means to have an innovative and experimental frame of mind. The author cautions us to not avoid risk nor choose what is always safe. The author recommends not to be too predictable but to embrace and adapt to change. Swoboda encourages us to find problems to solve and to go ahead and do what others say cannot be done. The author reminds readers that they should not be afraid to get their hands dirty, but that they also can be always looking for continuous improvement in the process.

As we turn our vision into action through experimentation, we can also consider how we might collaborate with others. We will certainly have our own leadership strengths to leverage; however, we will also have weaknesses and limitations of which we should be mindful. Lockwood and Papke (2018) encourage a collaborative process known as co-creation which increases idea-generation, broadens information-sharing and produces more effective problem-solving. Chapter 5 also offers concrete ways of collaborating toward a shared social transformation vision. Collaboration certainly has its benefits from a team and execution standpoint. During implementation, there will undoubtedly be obstacles and setbacks, so working closely in a team environment will also provide us with emotional support.

As we implement our plans with action and experimentation, consider how to be outcomes-based. Try to act on aspects that can deliver tangible results. There are different strategies to help one focus on outcomes. One such strategy is detailed by McChesney (n.d.) who describes the process as "The 4 Disciplines of Execution" for Franklin Covey (see: franklincovey.com/the-4-disciplines). For our social innovation purposes, Discipline 1 and 2, outlined below, are the most essential.

Discipline 1 is "the discipline of *focus*. Exceptional execution starts with narrowing the focus — clearly identifying what must be done" (original emphasis). This discipline recognizes the importance of prioritizing the most important goals. In fact, the author encourages the selection of one "WIG" (Wildly Important Goal), and to focus on achieving that rather than multiple goals at the same time. An important concept of this discipline is having a quantifiable timeline for accomplishment. A WIG needs a result that is measurable and a date by which it will be achieved.

Discipline 2 is "the discipline of *leverage*. 80% of your results will come from 20% of your activities [...]. [N]ot all actions are created equal. Identify and act on the activities with the highest leverage" (McChesney, n.d., original emphasis) The author describes two key metrics: lag and lead measures which help track our goals. Lag measures are those we can't do anything about as they are already in the past. Lead measures target the actions that can influence the lag measure. We need to remember that as we implement our plan with action, we need to narrow down our goals to focus on one high-priority goal that can be expressed with a measurable result and timeline. We can then leverage lead measures to influence the lag measure goal.

Furthermore, failure is a real and significant part of the process of action and experimentation. Wooditch (2019) reassures us that achievement is on the other side of failure. The author describes the concept of failing forward, which involves distancing ourselves from the negative emotions of failure and instead reacting logically and strategically. Wooditch also outlines the concept of being rejection-proof, whereby we are instructed to leverage the rejections and failures that surface into forward momentum, rather than dismissing or running away from them. Moreover, King (2022) reminds us that we are not our failures. The author encourages humour and authenticity in the face of failure, while using rejection as motivation to move forward.

To leverage failures in order to move forward, we need to remain focused on the progress made. Hardy and Sullivan (2021) describe a measurement system known as "The Gap and the Gain." The theory is to live in the gain and stay out of the gap. This means embracing the progress (the gain) we have made up to the current point, as opposed to being discouraged by what is still missing (the gap). The authors challenge us to interpret our past experiences with a sense of hope and optimism. As we experiment with action, we keep in mind that failures will undoubtedly come. However, instead of letting failure be a barrier, we can use our failure as fuel for growth.

Reflection Questions

Before reading the next section, take some time to reflect on these questions:

1. What is one "Wildly Important Goal" for your vision?
2. How could you plan for it in a quantifiable manner using a timeline?
3. What are the lead measures that will help influence your goal?
4. Who could you connect with for co-creation and starting a collaborative process?
5. How could you mentally prepare for impending failures and leverage them for growth?

EXPLORING A CASE STUDY

As inspiration, the following case study explores applications from GRADVision, a partnership between the Graduate Leadership Institute and the Office of Social Innovation at Toronto Metropolitan University (Graduate Leadership Institute, 2023). The initiative was an experiential leadership program that provided an opportunity for graduate students to consider transformative change solutions for social issues. This program was established in 2022, in recognition that higher education institutions had the resources to nurture the leadership roles that graduate students could be playing in addressing societal needs. The program consisted of a series of professional development workshops which offered a space for reflection and skill development so as to enhance the students' leadership potential so that they might be better able to contribute to meaningful change through their professional practices, be it their academic research, employment or community engagement.

There were several learning outcomes of the GRADVision program. By the end of the program, participants were able to: understand their core values; articulate their leadership purpose; identify societal needs or challenges; develop a vision for positive change; and begin to work toward vision implementation practices. The GRADVision program received tremendous feedback from its graduate student participants. Adefioye (2023), a graduate student and founder of a non-profit organization that provides empowerment and mentorship programs to Black immigrant women and youth, commented:

> It was a very good experience because I was able to strengthen my leadership skills. I was able to understand my core values better. I was able to also do a lot of reflections about my priorities. [...] One thing I've been doing since I took the program is to continue to develop empathy as we continue [with] the community impact work.

Additionally, Mounsef (2023), a filmmaker who created a documentary that tells the stories of families seeking justice and social change in his home country, described how:

> GRADVision really gave me a push to battle my fears and to take that risk because it was for a greater good. The vision statement was always something that we'd go back to. It was always this constant reminder and motivator of what we were doing and why we were doing it. We all have something we want to change. We all have a problem we want to solve and GRADVision offers that in the best way possible.

At the beginning of this chapter, we were invited to fully engage in this learning journey, to not only read this chapter from an academic perspective but also from a lens of personal reflection and application. In summary, we learned how to discover our core values, craft our leadership purpose, identify societal challenges, create a vision for change and turn vision into action. Our next step, now, is to take these lessons of personal transformation and become leaders of positive social change.

REFERENCES

Adefioye, A. (2023). *Testimonials*. Graduate and Postdoctoral Studies, Toronto Metropolitan University. www.torontomu.ca/graduate/graduate-leadership-institute/impact-results/

Brown, B. (2023). *Dare to lead: List of values*. [Website]. www.brenebrown.com/resources/dare-to-lead-list-of-values/

Cashman, K. (2017). *Leadership from the inside out: Becoming a leader for life*. Berrett-Koehler.

Covey, S.R. (2020). *The 7 habits of highly effective people: 30th anniversary edition*. Simon & Schuster.

Falke, K. (2022). *Lead well: 10 steps to successful and sustainable leadership*. Lioncrest Publishing.

Goodchild, M. (2021). Relational systems thinking: That's how change is going to come, from our Earth Mother. *Journal of Awareness Based Systems Change, 1*(1), 75–103.

Graduate Leadership Institute. (2023). *GRADVision* www.torontomu.ca/graduate/graduate-leadership-institute/grad-vision/.

Hardy, B., & Sullivan, D. (2021). *The gap and the gain: The high achievers' guide to happiness, confidence, and success*. Hay House Business.

Herold, C. (2018). *Vivid vision: A remarkable tool for aligning your business around a shared vision of the future*. Lioncrest Publishing.

Keyser, J. (2019). *You don't need to be ruthless to win: The art of badass selfless service*. Lioncrest Publishing.

King, A.T. (2022). *Failure rules: The 5 rules of failure for entrepreneurs, creatives, and authentics*. Lioncrest Publishing.

Kouzes, J., & Posner, J. (2017). *The leadership challenge: How to make extraordinary things happen in organizations*. John Wiley & Sons, Inc.

Lockwood, T., & Papke, E. (2018). *Innovation by design: How any organization can leverage design thinking to produce change, drive new ideas, and deliver meaningful solutions*. Career Press, Inc.

Mounsef, E. (2023). *Testimonials*. Graduate and Postdoctoral Studies, Toronto Metropolitan University. www.torontomu.ca/graduate/graduate-leadership-institute/impact-results/

Renshaw, B. (2018). *Purpose: The extraordinary benefits of focusing on what matters most*. LID Publishing.

Scott, J. (2019). *It's never just business: It's about people*. Lioncrest Publishing.

Spodek, J. (2019). *Initiative: A proven method to bring your passions to life (and work)*. Greenwich Lane Books.

Stanley, A. (2023). *The promise of visioneering*. Leadercast. [Website]. leadercast.com/the-promise-of-visioneering/

Swoboda, C. (2020). *The innovator's spirit: Discover the mindset to pursue the impossible*. Fast Company Press.

Wooditch, B. (2019). *Fail more: Embrace, learn, and adapt to failure as a way to success*. McGraw Hill Education.

Glossary

ALPHA-BETA-SIGMA MYTHOLOGY draws on debunked research on wolf hierarchies to describe masculinity, using the terms "alpha," "beta," "sigma" and "omega." These terms circulate online in men's rights extremist groups. An "alpha" is the lead, dominant wolf; a "beta" is a follower, an "omega" is at the bottom of the pack and often bullied; and a "sigma" is a "lone wolf." The changing science has not stopped groups like incels from using this terminology as a mode of self-validation, and the terms have even made their way into popular culture, largely divorced from their origin in such spaces.

ANTAGONISTIC COOPERATION is a process and/or expression that, on the one hand, seeks to include and attend to the most discordant voices while seeking, on the other hand, to work together to reach common goals. Rather than the discordance being seen as fragments, it is argued that it is enriching to a person's identity and art.

ARTS-BASED is an educational approach that integrates various art forms, activities and experiences as central components to enhance learning, creativity and critical thinking skills. It involves artistic processes like conceptualization, creating and performing. It also includes fostering active learning and reflective observation of an art form among students so as to encourage self-expression and imaginative exploration.

CHAD refers, in incel cant, to the archetypical, ideal man. A "Chad" has wealth, a dominating attitude and a powerful status. He is an attractive man, muscular and confident, with thick hair and a chiselled jaw. Incels sometimes use common, racially stereotyped, male names to argue for the existence (or not) of non-white Chads.

COLLAGE is both an artistic process and a form of art. It is typically associated with the mixing of images (often pre-existing) in a single plane. It has been typically defined as the use of papers, including manufactured images, with glue-based adhesive. Collage as an art form has been associated with decorative arts, deconstruction, process art, political art, feminist art and identity-focused art. Collage has a wide variety of definitions, often based on the artist's method, as well as intent for the practice. In a contemporary context, collage has expanded greatly to include work shown in pop-up shows and studio visits, and on the internet, mainly through social media.

COMMUNITY ENGAGED LEARNING AND TEACHING (CELT) is a pedagogical approach that integrates academic instruction with active and meaningful participation in the community. Emphasizing transformative learning, this approach facilitates experience that challenges assumptions, encourages critical reflection and promotes personal and societal change. It aims to empower students to become socially responsible, civically engaged, culturally aware individuals by having them participate in and contribute to the wider community. This engagement, in turn, fosters their academic and personal growth through experiential and reflective processes.

CONTENTIOUS POLITICS is a term that describes the use of disruptive techniques to make a political point. Contentious politics can also be processes and agreements that occur outside of traditional diplomatic or electoral means that usually have an impact on someone else's interests.

CRIP is a reclaimed word and form of self-identification used by some Disabled people. Like the use of "queer" in the 2SLGBTQ+ community, "crip" can be taken up as a politicized, Disabled identity.

DIALOGICAL refers to a communication process that includes the use of conversation or shared dialogue to explore the meaning of something.

DISABLED is a way of describing people with capacities that deviate from what is normally expected from an able-bodied person. The term is capitalized to indicate a critical understanding of Disability as an identity and to reflect an activist agenda toward social transformation.

ENVIRONMENTAL STEWARDSHIP is the responsible use and protection of the environment. This can be in the form of limiting harvesting and resource use to sustainable levels, as well as creating protected spaces. The concept of environmental stewardship is embedded in many Indigenous worldviews and treaties that ask us to share the land, take only what we need and leave enough for those who come after us.

EUROCENTRISM centres knowledge and culture in European culture or history, sometimes to the exclusion of a wider view of the world. In its extreme, eurocentrism regards European culture as preeminent.

FOREVER CHEMICALS is a term used for per- and polyfluorinated alkyl substances (PFAS) because of their extreme longevity in the environment. These chemicals contain multiple carbon fluoride bonds, which are the strongest bonds in organic chemistry. This strength means that these chemicals cannot be broken down under normal environmental conditions. Consequently, the use of PFAS in a variety of consumer and industrial products is leading to ever-increasing environmental contamination problems.

INCEL refers to an involuntary celibate man who believes himself to be victimized by what he and others like him describe as the "Western feminist social movement."

MAD is a reclaimed word and form of self-identification used by some people who experience mental health issues, including neurodivergence, and who interact with the mental health system, have experiences with psychiatrization and/or have histories of diagnoses.

NEOLIBERAL-ABLEISM is a framework used in critical disability theory to describe the ways neoliberal and ableist discourses interact to view crisis as an individual problem to be solved, making the assumption that each period of crisis is episodic and that a return to normative able-bodied life in between each episodic period of crisis is possible. This framework is informed by classic neoliberal values, such as independence and productivity.

NEOLIBERALISM is associated with economic policies of privatization, free trade, austerity and reductions in government spending on public works in order to increase the role of the private sector in society. The individual is one who is self-defined, autonomous and competitive; and one whose self-interest is elevated over social need.

NORMIE is a shortened form for "normal person" and is derogative. The term emerges and circulates mimetically, through online lingo, gamer culture and online men's rights extremist groups.

PARTICIPANT OBJECTIVATION works against the antimony between objectivist and subjectivist approaches to research and study. This approach to human affairs means that those who are observers are fully engaged in the exercise at the point of observation, rather than standing apart.

POSITIONALITY refers to an individual's lived experiences and social identities (e.g. gender, ethnicity, ability, profession, geographical location, etc.). The combination of these lived experiences and identities shapes how we perceive, understand and engage with the world around us and others. Positionality also shapes our perception of knowledge, perspectives and learning.

PRACTICE MOVEMENTS are seemingly unorganized and unrepresented collective actions that centre everyday activity and relationships. They mostly move for improved access to material goods; for representation or participation in typically exclusionary systems or institutions; and ultimately for the co-creation of livable lives.

PROVISIONAL COHERENCE is when one takes elements of a life, of a narrative, and combines them in order to reconstruct lives and history from fragments in such a manner that coherent thought is created, with the understanding that it will change over time.

SOCIAL ENTREPRENEUR in social innovation literature usually suggests that an individual is being smart and creative in addressing a particular social problem, and in so doing, is generating not only personal material benefit for themselves, but also benefit for a social group or community.

SOCIALLY ENGAGED ARTS (SEA) refers to collaboratively engaged art-making that integrates dialogue and social interactions with political and cultural aesthetics so as to centre social justice both in process and product.

SPECTACULAR(IZED) VIOLENCE refers to public acts or attempts to enact ideologically motivated mass violence where the act or attempt is mediated through methods of digital sharing (live-streamed, recorded, recirculated via news outlets), in addition to being visually dramatic and intentionally shocking or upsetting. This can also refer to the aestheticization and sensationalizing of visually dramatic or entertaining representations of violence.

STACY emerges from the cant of the incels. A "Stacy" is the desired, yet reviled, inaccessible woman. Stacy sleeps only with Chad but has a host of "beta" men in love with her. She uses her looks to manipulate men for money, goods and attention. Stacy is generally coded or explicitly represented as white, while racialized women are subjected to fetishizing representations under other terms.

STRUCTURAL POWER refers to the influence that people gain from the role they have within an institution. Roles that confer more structural power include being a faculty member as opposed to a student; working in philanthropy as opposed to working in the community sector; and being a staff member as opposed to an intern.

SYSTEMIC POWER refers to privileges accorded to people based on wider arrangements of power which favour one group over another to maintain social dominance, and/or access to resources for the privileged group.

TURTLE ISLAND is the name used by some Indigenous Peoples for North America (and sometimes, more broadly, for Earth). It is a reference to Indigenous creation stories common in communities across North America.

TWO-ROW WAMPUM is the oldest known treaty between some of the inhabitants of Turtle Island (the Haudenosaunee Confederacy) and newly arriving Europeans. The treaty establishes a framework of mutual respect and co-existence while emphasizing the distinctness and separateness of Haudenosaunee and European peoples and their independent affairs. Already extending for a period of more than four centuries, Two-Row Wampum established a friendship that is meant to endure through all the planet's natural cycles.

Index

Abramowitz, Emma (*Untitled*), 117–18
African villages, social innovation impacts, 15, 26–8
alpha-beta-sigma mythology, 65, 156
Amazon Ring,
    (dis)empowering narratives of, 58–62, 65, 76–8
    narratives of community safety/insecurity, 67–72, 76–7
    policing "disorderly behaviour," 60, 67–72, 76–7
    porch pirates and, 69
    profits from, 61–2, 68–71
    social innovation and, 58, 60–1, 67, 78
antagonistic cooperation, 108, 111, 156
anti-oppression, 15–16
anti-racism, 15, 39, 49
Arctic communities, 128
arts-based approaches, 38, 94, 105, 121, 156

Beam, Carl, 110
Black Healing Centre (BHC), 97–100
Black people, 71, 110, 119, 154
    creating healing spaces for, 97–100
    trauma/racism facing, 18, 23, 43, 97
Bourdieu, Pierre, 107
Braque, William Georges, 109
breakfast programs, 31
Butler, Judith, 107

capitalism,
    corporate profit motives under, 61–2, 68, 70
    flexibility/mobility and, 74–5
    mobilizing against, 37, 39, 41, 119
    social entrepreneurship in, 4, 15
    social relations under, 19, 64–7, 77
    see also neoliberalism
capitalist realism, 65–6
care collectives, 61, 75–6;
    see also collective care
Castellano, C.G., 37–8, 51
Chad, incel concept of, 65, 156, 159

charitable models,
    addressing social injustice through, 18–19, 31, 150
    social innovation and, 4–5, 25–6
chemistry education, 14, 158
    Indigenous ways of knowing and, 9, 128, 130, 138–9
    paradigm shifts in, 126–7, 131, 137, 140
    social justice/ethics and, 127–30, 136–8
children, 16, 136
    care systems for, 17–18, 23, 27, 31
    rights for, 147, 150
    see also youth
classism, 7, 39
coalition building, 4, 7, 39, 48
co-creation, 140, 159
    artistic, 37–8, 40–4, 51–5, 159
    collage, 113, 117
    community care, 74
    concept of, 10, 151–2
    social innovation and, 4–7, 129
Cohen, Sue (*Lockers Are Home*), 48
collaborative governance, 81–2, 87, 90–1, 99–100
collage,
    appropriation and, 109–10, 121
    community installations of, 47, 114–16, 118
    concept and history of, 105, 107–9, 123, 156–7
    as pedagogy, 105–8, 111–13, 115–20, 122–3
    social change/activism and, 9, 105–10, 114, 117–23
    types/various processes of, 109, 119–21, 123
collective action, 74
    arts-based, 40, 42, 47–8, 53, 159
    harmful power imbalances in, 59–60, 63, 66–9, 71–2
    social innovation as, 8, 58–60, 77
collective care, 67, 88, 99, 101
    Mad/Disabled, 58, 72, 75–8

162 INTERRUPTING INNOVATION

socially engaged arts-based, 36–7, 40,
42–7, 52
state/institutional care versus, 72, 74–5
see also care collectives
collective identity,
practice movements and, 40, 42, 47–8
social innovation and, 54
colonialism,
arts-based critiques of, 37–8, 42, 44,
51–2, 119
social innovation and, 4, 7, 16, 126,
129–30
systemic violence of, 42, 73
community engaged learning and teaching
(CELT), 88, 106, 113, 157
community safety, narratives of,
class-based security versus, 19, 68–71
collective actions based on, 66–9
surveillance amid, 59–60, 62, 65, 68–71,
76
Concordia University, 81, 88, 90–4, 97–8
Community Care Practitioners
Program, 99–100
contentious politics, 39, 43, 157
corporate influence,
in higher education, 8, 10
narratives of community safety, 67–9, 72
organizational design, 85–6
in social innovation, 58–9, 61–2
Covey, Franklin, 152
Covey, Stephen, 144
COVID-19 pandemic, 69, 81
artistic endeavours amid, 42–3, 53–4,
109–12, 115
Crawford, Adam, 71
Create Resist, 112, 114, 123
creativity,
in governance, 81, 92
importance in social innovation, 5–6,
17, 94, 148
research on, 5–7
socially engaged arts and, 38–40, 45,
51–5, 94, 156
crip, concept of, 75, 157

Daniels, Jerry, 138
Danner, Jordan (*Untitled*), 113
decolonial thinking/activism, 4
arts-based, 39, 41–2, 49, 51–2
decolonization,
of education systems, 16, 126, 129–30

democracy, 28, 41
governance and, 28, 84, 86, 101, 115
social, 49, 112
De Vitt, Jess (*Intrusive Thoughts /
An Invitation*), 42–4
dialogical communication, 39, 41, 47, 52–4,
157
Direct Funding Program (Ontario), 60, 72,
76–8
Disability Rights movement, 60, 72, 76, 147
Disabled people,
neoliberalism impacts on, 60, 63, 72–3,
77, 158
notion of, 157
user-directed versus institutional care
of, 58, 60–3, 72–8
see also Direct Funding Program
Disciplines of Execution (Franklin Covey),
152

Edwards, Nigel, 42–3
elders, care for, 16, 21–2, 27
empowerment,
class-based, 19, 68–71
collective action and, 58, 72, 75–8
false notions of, 58–62, 65, 72, 76–8
social innovation and, 16, 39–40,
59–60, 95
student/academic, 134, 150, 154, 157
entrepreneurship,
connecting innovation with, 2, 4–5, 94
neoliberal capitalist notion of, 4, 8, 28,
62, 71
social, *see* social entrepreneurs
environmental stewardship, 128, 132, 137,
139, 157
epistemologies, 30
Indigenous/decolonial, 4, 51–2
socially engaged arts and, 55, 113, 119–21,
123
eurocentrism, 19, 131, 139–40, 157

financial aid, student, 1–2
Fisher, Mark, 65
forever chemicals (PFAS), 129–30, 137–8, 158
Foucault, Michel, 38
Fry, Charlotte (*happy juice*), 121–2

Gap and the Gain (Hardy and Sullivan), 153
Gibb, Camilla, 115–16
Gilling, Daniel, 69–70

Goodchild, M., 4
governance,
    accountability in, 85–6, 88, 90–1, 97, 101
    democratic, 28, 84, 86, 101, 115
    dynamic, 82, 86–8, 97, 101
    self-, 84–6
    sociocratic, 82, 86–7
GRADVision program, 153–4
Gramsci, Antonio, 41
Happier Human (website), 147
Haughton, Hebony (*How They See Us*),
    119–20
Healing Through Art Days, 97, 99–100
Hear Us! (artistic endeavour), 46–8
Helguera, Paulo, 39
Herbert, Steve, 71
home, notions of, 19, 67
    art about, 46–8
    see also homelessness; housing
homelessness, 16
    as aesthetic problem, 19–21, 60
    arts-based representations of, 47–8
    perceptions of, 19–22, 48, 71
    as social problem, 6, 18–19, 22
homo securitas, 71
hooks, bell, 36, 38
housing,
    struggles to find secure, 2, 4, 16, 19, 47
    supportive, 19, 31
    see also home; homelessness

incels,
    "lay down and rot" (LDAR), 63–7, 77
    misogynistic/wounded orientation of,
        59, 63, 65–7, 156, 158–9
    online communities of, 58–9, 61–7
Indigenous people, 88, 127, 160
    art by/with, 50, 110
    Knowledge integration into STEM, 128,
        130–3, 139–40
    trauma/systemic violence facing, 18,
        23–5, 73
    treaty obligations, settler, 4, 132, 138–9,
        160
    worldviews of, 4, 44, 132–3, 138–9, 157
individualism,
    collective resistance to, 64, 75
    fallacy of, 27–9
    neoliberalism and, 10, 62, 65
    social innovation and, 5, 131
    socially engaged art versus, 38, 52

social problems and, 18, 23–4
inequities,
    collective action to counter, 40–1, 54,
        82, 97, 99
    financial/economic, 2, 10, 41, 74
    perpetuating structural, 16–17, 20, 40,
        82
    social innovation and, 25–7, 29, 71, 89
Initiative-Action-Passion cycle, 150
institutions, 18
    higher education (HEIs), 3, 7–8, 54, 109,
        133, 153
    neoliberalism and, 8, 75
    oppressive conditions in, 21, 23, 72–3,
        76, 133, 135–6
    organizing outside of, 39–40, 54, 74–6
    social innovation to counter, 58, 61, 77,
        82–4, 88–90, 159
    social problems in/from, 6–7, 66, 160

Kentridge, William, 107–8, 117–19

leadership, 11
    collaborative, 28, 40, 88–91
    of marginalized communities, 7, 44, 51,
        54–5, 88–90
    organizational design and, 84–6, 101
    purpose, crafting, 142–4, 145–9, 151–4
    transdisciplinary, 106, 111
learning organizations, 158
Li, Jennifer (*Dear Google*), 122–3
logocentric thinking, 117, 123
Lombardo, Charlotte, 37, 53

MacDonald, Logan (*Medicine Wheel
    Garden*), 49–50
Mad people,
    neoliberalism impacts on, 60, 63, 72–3,
        77, 158
    self-identification as, 158
    user-directed versus institutional care
        of, 58, 60–3, 72–8
Making With Place (MWP),
    art projects, 46, 48–51
    focus/research of, 36–7, 42–4, 47, 53–4
    Queering Place emergence, *see Queering
        Place*
    see also practice movements; socially
        engaged arts
Malatjie, Portia, 110
marginalized communities, 49, 131

164 INTERRUPTING INNOVATION

centring perspectives of, 81, 95, 106, 112–14, 119, 150
leadership of, 7, 44, 51, 54–5, 88–90
mobilizing while living on "edge," 36, 38–41, 63, 119–21, 123
social innovation impacts on, 22, 25–7, 61, 100
market-based approaches, 68
neoliberalism and, 62, 64
social innovation and, 4, 15–16, 20, 24, 84
Marrast, Logan, 45
masculinity,
confronting toxic, 45–6
incel, 59, 63, 65–6, 156
Mensah, Suzie (*An Invitation*), 43–4
mental health, 64, 147, 158
Black, 97, 99
child and youth, 17
homelessness and, 19, 21–2
mentorship, 45, 146–7
programs, 8, 89, 151, 154
Mignolo, Walter, 41–2, 49, 51–2
misogyny, 59, 63–7, 77
mutual aid/support, 88
artistic collaboration and, 44, 49, 55
disabled/crip communities', 75

neoliberal ableism, 74–5, 158
neoliberalism,
anxiety under, 2, 23, 43, 65, 67
concept of, 10, 158
entrepreneurship, concept in, 4, 8, 15, 26–8, 62, 71
individualism in, 10, 62, 65
inequities under, 2, 10, 16–17, 20, 40–1, 74
institutional reinforcement of, 8, 75
Mad/Disabled people, impacts on, 60, 63, 72–7, 158
mobilizing against, 37, 39, 41, 58, 119
negative impacts of, 2, 10, 16–17, 20, 40–1, 60–5, 74
social innovation and, 10, 28–30, 58–9, 61–2, 68
surveillance amid, 59–60, 62, 65, 68–71, 76
see also capitalism
neoliberal subjects, 66–7, 71–2, 74
networked communities,
incel, 64–5, 67, 77

technology for, 63, 65, 67–8, 107
networks, community,
disabled people's care, 63, 72, 74–5
social innovation/change, 3, 7, 39–40, 88–9, 99
utility of, 27–31
normie, concept of, 63, 158
Novak, Phyllis, 37, 53

O'Meally, Robert, 108, 119
oppression,
communities countering, 6–7, 15, 36, 52, 55
systemic/state-based, 7, 18, 23, 42, 73, 93
see also anti-oppression
organizational design,
accountability in, 85–6, 88, 90–1, 97, 101
history and theory of, 85–8
leadership in, 84–6, 101
power relations and, 82–6, 89, 93, 95, 128
Orupabo, Frida, 110, 119
Ozyonum, Ezgi, 93–4

participant objectification, 107, 158–9
per- and polyfluorinated substances (PFAS), *see* forever chemicals
Peterson, Tom, 148
Petrunia, Lisa (*Safe Landing*), 48
Picasso, Pablo, 109
Piepzna-Samarasinha, Leah Lakshmi, 73, 78
place, 4, 99
artistic contemplation on, 38, 42–4, 54
queering, 49–51
positionality, 7, 93, 133, 159
power relations,
academic, 88, 107, 128, 134–5
collective action/identity and, 27, 37–8, 41, 48, 51–3
common contestations of, 6, 16–17, 55, 95, 146
incel perceptions of, 59, 63, 66–7
organizational design and, 82–6, 89, 93, 95, 128
perpetuation of hegemonic, 4–5, 8, 14, 20, 70–3
social innovation sharing/shifting, 3–7, 11, 82–3, 86–92, 100–1
structural, 93, 95–6, 160
transforming dominant, 60–2, 78, 122

Index   165

practice movements, 40, 159
  socially engaged arts as, 36–7, 41–2,
    52–3, 108–9, 123
  see also social movements
provisional coherence, 108, 111–12, 159

racism,
  anti-Black, 43, 46, 97, 108
  neoliberal capitalism and, 39, 73
  as social problem, 7, 9, 16–17, 21
  systemic, 46, 65, 97
  see also anti-racism
radical belonging, 37, 42, 49, 53
Rahman, Nafija (SHIFT community
  member), 81–2, 95–6
Reconstructions of Home (artistic endeavour), 46–8
Reed, Emmet (Being Seen), 48
relationality, 135
  community contributions through, 21,
    29
  importance in social innovation, 2, 4,
    7, 27–9
  socially engaged arts and, 37, 39–44, 47,
    51–2, 54–5
responsibilization, 71
  concept of, 10–11
  collective versus individuated, 60, 68, 72
  Disabled support and, 60, 72, 76–8

Schumann, Peter, 3
science education,
  critical thinking/positionality in, 132–5
  evaluation in, 135–7
  importance of innovation in, 3, 14,
    126–7
  Indigenous perspectives in, 128, 130–3,
    138–40
  objectivity, false notion of, 127, 131–3,
    135–40
  social justice in, 127–9, 130–1, 134, 140
  see also chemistry education
sexism, 7, 9, 39; see also misogyny
Sheppard, Kate, 114–15
SHIFT Centre for Social Transformation,
  accountability in, 85–6, 88, 90–1, 97, 101
  decision-making processes, 81, 83,
    86–9, 91–8
  ecosystem of, 81–3, 89, 91–3, 97, 100–1
  governance model/hub, 81–3, 89–92,
    94–7, 100

principles of, 90, 93–7
relationships and projects of, 81, 88–91,
  97–100
sharing/shifting of power, 82–4, 86–92,
  100–1
steering committee initiatives, 81–2, 88,
  91–2, 94–6
see also organizational design
Simpson, Jeffrey (Decriminalize), 114
SKETCH Working Arts, 37, 44, 55–6
So, Ada (Connections), 115–16
social, the, see the social
social entrepreneurs, 26–8, 159
social innovation,
  aesthetics of, 14–15, 26, 29–31, 54, 123
  attempts to depoliticize, 4, 17, 26–7
  concepts of, 22, 26–7, 30–1, 39
  as contextual/relational, 2, 4, 7, 22, 24–5,
    27–9
  co-optation of, 58–61, 68, 72, 77–8
  critical assessments of, 2, 4, 10, 58–62,
    132–4, 137
  empowerment narratives of, see
    empowerment
  growing interest in, 3–4, 11, 26, 39, 84
  innovation versus, 14, 16
  negative sides of, 6, 15–16, 26–31, 59, 63,
    77, 82
  amid neoliberalism, see neoliberalism
  political construction of, 17, 30, 55
  rejection of branding of, 15–16
  sensory context, 16, 19–20, 24–7, 30–1
  transformative, see transformation,
    social
social innovators, 17
  fallacy of, 16, 26–31
social justice, 82, 105, 159
  community struggles for, 36, 99
  definition of, 5
  in science education, 127–9, 130–1, 134,
    140
  social innovation and, 1–7, 30, 58–9,
    126, 142–4, 147–9
socially engaged arts (SEA),
  concept of, 37–8, 159
  continuum in, 42, 52–3
  as practice movement, 36–7, 41–2, 52–3
  relationality and, 37, 39–44, 47, 51, 54–5
  transformative nature of, 38, 49
social media, 10, 23
  collage work on, 109–11, 114, 119–21, 157

166 INTERRUPTING INNOVATION

social movements, 15
  art practice movements as, *see* practice
    movements
  Disability Rights, 60, 76
  feminist, 59, 158
  social innovation and, 7, 22, 58, 61, 78
  transformative, 29, 78, 85, 89
social problems,
  aesthetics of, 19–21
  attempted solutions worsening, 17–18,
    20, 24–8
  benefits of, 16–17, 22, 30–1
  concepts of, 18–21, 28–9, 62
  examples of, 17–19, 23–5, 26–8
  seeming intractability of, 3–5, 16–17,
    22–4
  social innovation and, 16, 24–8, 30–1,
    39, 159
  wicked, 5–7
sociocracy, 82, 86–7
Soken-Huberty, Emmaline, 147
solidarity,
  building, 4, 36–8, 49, 71–2
  social innovation and, 4, 7, 22
  socially engaged art and, 49, 53, 55
Sousa, Wellington, 41
Spade, Dean, 41
spectacular(ized) violence, 63, 66–7, 159
Stacy, incel concept of, 65, 159
structural power, 93, 95–6, 160
student loans/debt, 1–2
surveillance, 20
  community safety narratives and,
    59–60, 62, 65, 68–71, 76
  (dis)empowerment through, 58–62,
    65, 76–8
systemic power, 66, 93, 160

The Bentway, 46–7
The Good Guise (*My Public Living Room*),
  45–6
*The Guise Guide: A Radical Care Zine for
  Racialized Men*, 46
the social,
  as central in social innovation, 16, 21–2,
    24–6, 29–31
  problems from ignoring, 24, 28–9
Toronto Metropolitan University (TMU),
  112, 153
  art exhibits at, 111, 113–16, 118, 120–2
  faculty at, 106, 127–9

  student debt at, 1–2
transformation, social, 157
  art-based mobilizing for, 38, 41, 45–6,
    49–52, 105–6
  concept of, 89, 95
  harmful, 63–4, 66–7, 75–8
  institutional initiatives for, 8, 58, 60–1,
    82–3, 86, 89–101
  science-based, 126–7, 134–5
  social innovation and, 2–8, 30, 58, 82–3,
    89, 142–3
  trauma and, 24–5
trauma,
  concept and ubiquity of, 22–3
  perceptions/treatment of, 23–4, 28, 97
  racial, 23, 97
  social innovation and, 24–5
Trypis, Olympia (*Medicine Mobiles /
  Dreamcatcher Mobiles*), 43–4
Turtle Island, 128, 160
Two-Row Wampum, 4, 139, 160
values,
  finding core, 142–7, 149–51, 154
  imagined community, 52, 61, 69
  neoliberal capitalist, 4, 19, 21–2, 27, 29,
    158
  science field, 107–8, 135
  social innovation and, 4, 29, 88–92, 94,
    100
Vaughan, R.M., 111–12, 118, 120
violence,
  colonial, 42, 52, 73
  gendered, 16, 23, 27
  incel, 59, 66–7
  neoliberal capitalism and, 39
  social innovation and, 15, 45–6
  spectacular, *see* spectacular(ized)
    violence
  systemic, 16–18, 22, 73–4
  trauma and, *see* trauma

Walsh, C.E., 41–2, 49, 51–2
Weber, Max, 135
white supremacy, 19, 39, 73, 156, 159
wicked social problems, 5–7

Young, Kristen, 97
youth, 71
  Black and Indigenous, 18, 25, 154
  socially engaged arts for, 25, 36–7, 44–5
  service system negotiation, 17–18, 20, 31